5-Minute Mug Cakes

Nearly 100 Yummy Microwave Cakes

Jennifer Lee

Race Point
PUBLISHING

Race Point Publishing
An imprint of Quarto Publishing Group USA Inc.
276 Fifth Avenue, Suite 205
New York, New York 10001

RACE POINT PUBLISHING and the distinctive Race Point Publishing
logo are trademarks of Quarto Publishing Group USA Inc.

ISBN: 978-1-937994-98-3

Library of Congress Cataloging-in-Publication Data is available

Text: Jennifer Lee
Photography: Jon Meade (www.jonmeadephotography.com)
Food Styling: Michelle Lo
Editorial Director: Jeannine Dillon
Project Manager: Erin Canning
Copyeditor: Lindsay Herman
Cover Designer: Heidi North

Printed in China

1 3 5 7 9 10 8 6 4 2

Contents

Introduction

Did you know you can make a delicious cake in *just 1 minute*? Well, you can! Mug cakes are just what they sound like: single-serving desserts prepared directly in a mug and then cooked in the microwave. Most recipes in this book can be prepared in **less than five minutes**. They are instant desserts—perfect for those days when you just need a quick, scrumptious, sweet snack that requires little effort and few ingredients.

I first forayed into the world of mug cakes a few years ago. I was hesitant to make one for a very long time because the reviews for mug cakes were often negative: *rubbery, dry, eggy*. Then one day, I came across a recipe promising a moist chocolate mug cake. I was curious and gave it a try: It wasn't bad, but I thought it could be better. So I began to experiment with mug cakes in my kitchen. I finally came up with a mug cake I really loved: a heavenly Nutella chocolate mug cake. I posted it on my food blog, *Kirbie's Cravings*. From there, things just took off.

My mind was churning out mug cake ideas faster than I could make them. My readers were equally enthusiastic, offering up tasty suggestions. People started referring to me as "the Mug Cake Girl" and before I knew it, I had more than 100 mug cake recipes posted on my food blog. Many of my mug cakes have even been shared in national publications. Early on, several people suggested that I turn my mug cake endeavors into a book, and when I was approached by a publisher to do so, I finally began to take the idea seriously.

My mug cakes take a **back-to-basics** approach, eliminating all unnecessary ingredients (which also often results in the recipes being *eggless*). This means that my cakes are *not* dry, rubbery, eggy, or high in calories—all common problems that plague mug cakes. Instead, the flavors are pure as can be.

This book contains 100 scrumptious mug cake recipes for all sorts of occasions and tastes. Many of the treats in this book are brand-new, never-before-published recipes. There are much-loved classics like Cookie Cakes, Brownie Cakes, and Fruity Cakes. For the kid-at-heart or kid in your home, you'll find nostalgic concoctions like the Hostess Cake, S'mores Cake, PB&J Cake, and Hot Cocoa Cake, as well as adorable holiday-themed recipes with festive flavors like pumpkin, gingerbread, eggnog, and even Halloween candy! I've also transformed sweet breakfast favorites into mug cake form—try the decadent Maple Syrup Pancake or French Toast Cake, the Blueberry Muffin Streusel or the Honey Swirl. There are boozy cakes, coffee and tea cakes, and yes, even savory cakes for those moments when you *don't* crave something sweet!

For people with dietary restrictions, I've created recipes for Gluten-Free Cakes and Skinny Cakes (containing less than 200 calories), because no one should ever be deprived of their sweet-tooth fix. And finally, for the optimum insta-cake experience, you'll find recipes requiring only four ingredients or less—no special trip to the supermarket required! Each mug cake has been tested, re-tested, and tested again, to ensure that only the best ended up in this book.

Perhaps you're too busy or too exhausted to make an entire cake. Maybe it's late at night and you have a sudden, unrelenting craving for a slice of cake, yet there are no baked goods within reach. You might be cramming for a test or working on a big project, and you just *really* need an instant pick-me-up. Or maybe you've suffered the cruel misfortune of a broken-down oven. Whatever the circumstances, these mug cake recipes offer a quick and satisfying solution: With minimal prep and cleanup, they are great for virtually any situation, whether you're a baking novice or a magician in the kitchen, and whether you're snacking solo or serving guests. I hope you have a great time trying out these easy recipes, and I hope you reach for this book whenever the mug cake mood strikes.

Mug Cake Essentials

I use a **back-to-basics** approach with my mug cakes, eliminating all unnecessary ingredients to ensure the purest flavors and healthier cakes. You'll notice that the ingredient lists are quite short and that most recipes don't call for egg (see "Eggs" on page xii to find out why).

Most of the ingredients used in these recipes are readily available at grocery stores in the U.S. **Do** try to use all the ingredients listed and make sure that all ingredients are properly measured out. If you're missing something you need, **do not** simply leave it out or replace it with a similar substitute—the recipe will not turn out well. For example, when a recipe calls for all-purpose flour, don't try to substitute wheat flour instead; likewise, if an ingredient list specifies "store-bought" peanut butter, don't swap it for the natural kind.

Similarly, try not to "estimate" measurements. These recipes work with a very small amount of ingredients, so inaccuracies in measurements make a huge impact in the result. To prevent any mug cake mishaps, please take a close look at your recipe's ingredients and measurements before you begin.

Ingredients

Here are some of the basics you'll need for almost every recipe in the book.

Flour

Wheat flours (all-purpose, cake flour, and bread flour) are distinguished by the level of proteins contained in them. As a result, you cannot substitute flours without having to tweak other ingredients in the recipe.

When measuring out flour, be careful not to "pack" the flour. First spoon the flour into your measuring spoon or cup and then level it off with a knife. Flour becomes compacted when it is packaged and sold. Packing occurs when you directly scoop the flour from the bag into your measuring cup—this results in too much flour and will make your cakes dry and tough.

All-purpose flour: The majority of recipes in this book use all-purpose flour (often referred to as *plain flour*), which is a type of wheat flour with a medium amount of proteins.

I tried to create as many recipes as possible using all-purpose flour since it is the most common flour in people's kitchens. All-purpose flour is usually sold in two varieties: bleached or unbleached. Either one will work for the recipes in this book.

Cake flour: A few recipes in this book specify the use of cake flour. Cake flour has a lower protein content and results in a tender texture and more delicate crumb.

Baking powder and baking soda

The majority of recipes call for baking powder or baking soda. Both baking powder and baking soda are leavening agents, producing carbon dioxide, which allows the baked goods to rise.

Make sure your baking powder and baking sodas are fresh. Both need to be replaced every few months or else they lose their effectiveness. If you haven't baked in a while and your cake just isn't rising, it's likely that your baking powder or baking soda needs to be replaced.

Please note: Even though both baking powder and baking soda are leavening agents, **they are not interchangeable**! Baking soda is sodium bicarbonate: It needs an acidic ingredient to interact with before it will release carbon dioxide. Baking powder is part sodium bicarbonate already mixed with an acidic element and a starch.

Sugar

In addition to being a sweetener, sugar also alters the moisture, texture, and structure of cakes. As a result, do not substitute the sugar specified in the recipe for another sweetener.

Granulated sugar: There are different kinds of granulated sugar, but for the purposes of this book, recipes that call for granulated sugar refer to *granulated white sugar*. This is the most common sugar found in people's pantries and used for cooking—often referred to as *regular sugar*, *white sugar*, or *table sugar*.

Brown sugar: Brown sugar is granulated sugar with molasses. Light brown sugar has a golden color and less molasses flavor. Dark brown sugar has a darker brown hue and a richer molasses flavor. Most of the recipes in this book that use brown sugar call for light brown sugar. While the recipes work better with light brown sugar, if you only have dark brown sugar at home, you can substitute for dark brown. A few recipes specify dark brown sugar to obtain the deeper molasses flavor.

Unlike flour, you do want the brown sugar to be packed when you measure it. To do so, scoop your measuring device directly into the brown sugar bag, scooping up a little more than the measuring cup or spoon can hold. Then use your fingers to pack it down, and level off with a knife if needed. When you turn out the brown sugar, it should hold the shape of the cup or spoon.

Brown sugar will harden if it is not stored in a tightly sealed container. If that happens, you can heat it up in the microwave for a few seconds to make it moist again.

Confectioners' sugar: Confectioners' sugar, or powdered sugar, is granulated sugar that has been ground to a smooth powder. It is usually mixed with cornstarch to prevent caking. It's often used to make frostings because it dissolves more easily.

Milk
Most of these recipes call for fat-free milk to make the cakes healthier. You can replace it with low-fat or whole milk, if you like. However, if a recipe specifies whole milk, do not try to substitute a low-fat or fat-free milk, as the cake is dependent on the fat from the whole milk.

Vegetable oil
Most of the traditional cakes in this book use vegetable oil. This refers to the common and generically labeled "vegetable oil" bottles in grocery stores. Vegetable oil is used because of its neutral flavor. Canola oil can also be used as a substitute. Avoid using olive oil and other similar oils because they have a distinct flavor that will alter the taste of the cakes.

Also avoid using melted butter instead of vegetable oil. Butter has a lesser fat content than vegetable oil so a direct substitution will lead to a dryer cake.

Butter
For the recipes that require butter, always use **unsalted** butter. Unsalted butter is generally used in baking because it gives you control of the salt content that goes into the dessert. Salted butters have varying amounts of salt added depending on the manufacturer, which can alter the taste of your baked goods.

Eggs

Eggs are actually absent from the ingredient list for the majority of these recipes, but I'm adding a section about them here to explain why. Many mug cake recipes suffer from a rubbery texture or eggy aftertaste, and the problem is the egg.

In general, eggs are pretty essential to baking. They act as thickeners, leaveners, and emulsifiers, provide structure, add moisture and fat, and contribute to taste and color. So it only seems natural that eggs would be needed in a mug cake.

The problem is that a mug cake is meant to be a single-serving dessert, so when you add a whole egg, it is simply too much—especially when entire cakes can be made with two or three eggs. There are ways to compensate for this problem. You can reduce the egg amount and use half-eggs for all the recipes, but having to split an egg every time you want a mug cake can be quite annoying. More commonly, recipes increase the quantity of all the other ingredients. However, this then defeats the purpose of having a one-serving dessert, because you end up with oversized cakes that can be close to a whopping 1,000 calories per serving.

After much trial and error, I managed to create mug cakes without the use of any egg at all. The cakes are still moist, light, and fluffy and they are much healthier without the fat content from an egg yolk. You'll find that some of these cakes have a looser crumb than a traditional cake because there is no egg to act as a binding agent—but since these cakes will be eaten out of a mug, they don't need to stand upright by themselves.

There are a few recipes in this book where the texture simply wouldn't be right without some egg in the batter. For example, what we think of as a "cookie" is largely dependent on its structure, so the cookie cakes do use a little bit of whisked egg.

Chocolate

The chocolate mug cakes in this book call for either semisweet chocolate chips, chopped chocolate, or unsweetened cocoa powder. Carefully review the following information before making any substitutions.

Semisweet chocolate chips: Most of the recipes use semisweet chocolate chips. These refer to the most common baking chocolate chips found in your grocery store and usually used for cookies. Normally, chocolate chips are not used for melting because of their lower cocoa butter content; but for the ease of these recipes, I developed them to work with melted chocolate chips.

You don't have to use standard chocolate chips. You can use any other form of semisweet chocolate, like semisweet baking chocolate bars (chopped), semisweet chocolate discs, or semisweet chocolate chunks. But please stick to using **semisweet** chocolate, otherwise the taste and texture of the cake will be affected. Also, please note that if you are using something other than standard-sized chocolate chips, you should weigh out the chocolate to make sure you get the right amount. Measuring out ¼ cup of standard-sized chocolate chips and ¼ cup large chocolate chunks will likely yield different weights simply because of the amount that fits into the measuring cup.

Be careful when melting the chips in the microwave. You don't want to overheat and burn the chocolate. I was able to heat my chocolate with cold milk at full power without any issues, but if you find your microwave is too strong, you can reduce the power level.

Chopped chocolate: A few recipes use chopped chocolate. Baker's brand baking chocolate is the easiest to use because the chocolates are conveniently divided into 1-ounce pieces. Make sure to use the type of chocolate specified in the recipe (for example, don't use unsweetened if the recipe calls for dark chocolate). If you have other chocolate bars in your pantry, you can use those instead, as long as they are the same type of chocolate specified. So, for example, if the recipe calls for chopped dark chocolate, and you have a giant dark chocolate bar sitting on the shelf, go ahead and use that instead of the "baking" dark chocolate.

Unsweetened cocoa powder: There are two types of unsweetened cocoa powder—Dutch-processed/alkalized cocoa and natural cocoa. Make sure you don't mistake unsweetened cocoa powder for the sweetened cocoa powder used to make hot chocolate. (The one recipe in this book that *does* use sweetened cocoa powder is the Hot Cocoa Cake on page 74, as stated in the ingredients).

Dutch-processed or alkalized cocoa powder has been treated with an alkalizing agent to reduce the acidity of the cocoa. It's usually darker in color, and it's used in the mug cake recipes because it has a more delicate flavor. Look for the label to say "Dutch-processed" or "processed with alkali." Usually this type of cocoa powder is not found at supermarkets and will need to be purchased at baking supply stores. If you only have natural cocoa in your kitchen, you can use it for a recipe that calls for Dutch-processed, but be aware that your cake may have a more bitter finish.

Natural cocoa tends to be bitter and will often be labeled "natural unsweetened" or have no label at all. This is usually the unsweetened cocoa found at supermarkets produced by popular brands like Hershey's and Ghirardelli. Natural cocoa is more acidic and leaves a bitter taste, which is why it's not used as often in baked goods—with the exception of recipes calling for baking soda (as discussed earlier, baking soda needs an acidic element to react with). If a recipe specifies natural cocoa, you cannot substitute it for Dutch-processed because the recipe is depending on the acidity of the natural cocoa.

Kitchen Equipment

The tools needed for these mug cakes are very basic, but please review this section before you begin, as it also provides tips and insights for the best mug cake-making experience.

Oversized mug

You will need a microwave-safe mug that can hold at least 12 ounces of liquid. I usually use mugs that hold between 12 and 16 ounces. A large mug is required to ensure that the batter stays within the mug when it is cooking and rising. You don't want it to overflow and make a mess in your microwave.

If you don't know how much liquid your mug holds, as a general rule, you don't want the cake batter to fill up more than half the mug. You can also measure your mug by filling it to the top with water and then pouring the water into a liquid measuring cup.

While your favorite oversized mug will likely work just fine, I've cooked with enough different mugs to be able to offer a few pointers for finding the optimal kind. The ideal mug will be **tall**, **curved**, with **thick walls**.

- **Why tall?** The height ensures that your cake does not overflow.
- **Why curved?** Curved walls allow you to thoroughly mix your ingredients without anything getting stuck in crevices at the bottom of the mug. When the interior is completely straight, flour is more likely to wedge itself into the sharp corners. If you have no choice but to cook with a straight mug, be sure to maneuver your whisk around to get all the flour stuck in the inner bottom ring.
- **Why thick?** Thick walls withstand heat better than thin ones. Mugs made of thin material sometimes overheat quickly, which can overcook or unevenly cook your cake.

NOTE: Most cakes in the photographs were cooked in smaller mugs so that you can clearly see the cake. Because all these cakes rise to different levels, I recommend using oversized mugs across the board so the batter doesn't spill over in your microwave. However, if you want to achieve the overflowing appearance you see in the photos, my suggestion is to first make the recipe in an oversized mug. Once you have an idea how high that specific cake will rise, you can start testing it in smaller mugs until you find the ideal one—where the cake will rise past the rim without the batter dripping everywhere in your microwave.

Measuring spoons

You'll need a set of measuring spoons to measure out the ingredients for these recipes. Use a set you know to be very accurate, or at least use the same set to measure out the entire recipe, even though this may mean you need to wash a spoon or two in between.

Unfortunately, not all measuring spoon sets are accurate, and if you end up using two different sets, you might end up with disappointing mug cakes. When making large cakes, the inaccuracy of the measuring spoon is usually minimal; but when you are working with such a small quantity of ingredients, precision becomes much more important. For example, a tablespoon that is slightly too big can add an extra ½ tablespoon of flour to the batter after a few scoops, which would make the mug cake much too dry. By using the same set, you will at least have the same ratios for your measurements.

Along the same lines, please try to be as accurate as possible when measuring your ingredients. When you are working with small amounts, eyeballing measurements will likely lead to cake mishaps. If you are working with sticky ingredients like a Nutella spread, try your best to get it all out of the spoon and into your mug. If you are working with loose ingredients like flour, make sure you don't pack the flour—just loosely scoop it up.

Small whisk

The recipes in this book require a small whisk to mix the batter: It should easily mix ingredients in the narrow confines of a mug, so a standard whisk will be too big. Small whisks cost only a few dollars and can be found in the baking aisle of grocery stores, specialty baking shops, and through online merchants like Amazon.

Small or mini whisks usually come in two sizes. You don't want to choose the tiny one that looks cute enough for a tea party, as it won't be sturdy or strong enough. Instead, pick the one that is slightly bigger. An ideal size is around 7 inches in length (including the handle), with a whisk portion that is slightly less than 1 inch wide and about 2½ inches long.

Note: You might wonder if a fork will work to mix the batter. I don't recommend it. While it is possible to mix with a fork, unless you have extremely powerful hand-mixing skills, you will end up with little lumps of flour in your finished cake—which are obviously not pleasant to eat. Spend the few bucks to buy a whisk and it'll save you a lot of time and energy.

Microwave

The cooking times given for the recipes in this book are based on the 1000-watt microwave in my kitchen, completed at the full power setting. Microwaves differ in wattage, so you may have to make some minor time adjustments or reduce the power setting. Sometimes the material of your mug can affect cooking time as well.

Most of the cakes will take about 1 minute to cook. If you have to adjust cooking time, make sure to add or subtract only **about 15 seconds at a time**. You want to be very careful not to overcook the cake. Once overcooked, it becomes hard, dry, or rubbery—and even a mere 15 seconds can make a huge difference. It is much better to *undercook* the cake than to overcook it, since the cake will continue to cook in the mug once you've removed it from the microwave to cool.

Chocoholic Mug Cakes

I think all dessert recipe books should have a dedicated section to chocolate. Eating chocolate produces feelings of euphoria that no other food can replicate. This is not a complete list of all the chocolate recipes in this book because a few of them fit better into other chapters, but here you'll find some of my most decadent and mouthwatering chocolate-based mug cake recipes, including Chocolate Lava, Cookies & Cream, and Salted-Caramel Chocolate.

Oh chocolate, how I love thee...

Original Chocolate Cake

This is my basic chocolate cake recipe. Do not let the simplicity fool you. It has a powerful chocolate flavor that completely satisfies chocolate cravings. The key is using melted chocolate instead of cocoa powder. Melting chocolate may seem like one step too many, but it's a painless process that takes less than one minute.

¼ cup (45g) semisweet chocolate chips

3 tbsp (45ml) fat-free milk

2 tbsp (15g) all-purpose flour

¼ tsp baking powder

½ tbsp (7.5ml) vegetable oil

1 Combine chocolate chips and milk in an oversized microwave-safe mug. Microwave for about 40 seconds. Mix with a small whisk until chocolate is completely melted.

2 Add flour, baking powder, and oil and whisk until batter is smooth.

3 Cook in microwave for about 1 minute. If cake is not done, heat an additional 15 seconds. Let cake cool a few minutes. Cake is best consumed while still warm or within a few hours of it being cooked.

Chocolate Lava Cake

Chocolate lava cake is an exquisite creation: *warm chocolate cake with a melted gooey center*. What's not to love? It is no wonder this dessert is so popular and shows up on practically every restaurant menu. With this recipe, there's no need to wait for a fancy dinner to indulge in this sinful dessert.

Note: This cake is best eaten while still warm, but be careful not to burn yourself because the melted chocolate center is quite hot.

¼ cup (45g) semisweet chocolate chips

3 tbsp (45ml) fat-free milk

2 tbsp (15g) all-purpose flour

¼ tsp baking powder

½ tbsp (7.5ml) vegetable oil

3 chocolate rectangles (0.4oz) from a plain 1.5-oz chocolate bar, like Hershey's milk or dark chocolate (each about 1 inch in width)

1 tsp confectioners' sugar, optional

1. Combine chocolate chips and milk in an oversized microwave-safe mug. Microwave for about 40 seconds. Mix with a small whisk until chocolate chips are completely melted.

2. Add flour, baking powder, and oil and whisk until batter is smooth.

3. Push the chocolate bar pieces into the center of the batter, until batter completely covers them.

4. Cook in microwave for about 1 minute. If cake is not done, heat an additional 15 seconds. Let cake cool a few minutes, and then sift a little confectioners' sugar on top. Cake is best consumed while still warm.

Chocolate Truffle Cake

What's better than regular chocolate cake? A cake made with chocolate truffles: luxurious, creamy, melt-in-your-mouth truffle chocolate pieces will give you one seriously decadent chocolate cake.

4 Lindt truffle balls, chopped in half (or 50g other chopped truffle chocolates)

3 tbsp (45ml) fat-free milk

2 tbsp (15g) all-purpose flour

¼ tsp baking powder

½ tbsp (7.5ml) vegetable oil

1   Combine chocolate and milk in an oversized microwave-safe mug. Microwave for about 40 seconds. Mix with a small whisk until chocolate is completely melted.

2   Add flour, baking powder, and oil and whisk until batter is smooth.

3   Cook in microwave for about 1 minute. If cake is not done, heat an additional 15 seconds. Let cake cool a few minutes. Cake is best consumed while still warm or within a few hours of it being cooked.

Chocolate Vanilla Marble Cake

Marble cakes are so lovely to look at, with their mesmerizing swirls. This cake takes a little more time because you need to make two separate batters and then swirl them together. But the end result is pretty as a picture—before you dig in.

4 tbsp (30g) all-purpose flour

¼ tsp baking powder

½ tbsp (7.5ml) plus ½ tbsp (7.5ml) vegetable oil

3 tbsp (45ml) fat-free milk

1 tbsp (12.5g) granulated sugar

⅛ tsp vanilla extract

½ tbsp (4g) unsweetened cocoa powder (Dutch-processed)

1   Combine flour, baking powder, ½ tablespoon oil, milk, and sugar in an oversized microwave-safe mug. Mix with a small whisk until batter is smooth.

2   Remove 2 tablespoons of the batter into a separate small bowl. Add vanilla to the batter in the bowl and whisk.

3   Add cocoa powder and remaining ½ tablespoon oil to the batter in the mug and whisk until smooth.

4   Add dollops of vanilla batter on top of the chocolate batter, then create the marbling effect: With a knife, simply draw multiple figure eights into the batter.

5   Cook in microwave for about 1 minute. If cake is not done, heat an additional 15 seconds. Let cake cool a few minutes. Cake is best consumed while still warm or within a few hours of it being cooked.

Cookies & Cream Cake

I don't know what it is about the appearance of cookies 'n' cream that just makes me giddy—perhaps it's the throwback to my childhood days. This cake starts with a white chocolate base, which is then mixed with crushed Oreo cookies. The end result is a cake studded with chocolate cookie crumbles and cream.

¼ cup (45g) white chocolate chips

3 tbsp (45ml) whole milk

4 tbsp (30g) all-purpose flour

¼ tsp baking powder

½ tbsp (7.5ml) vegetable oil

2 Oreo cookies

CREAM CHEESE FROSTING, optional (serves 2)

2 tbsp (28g) cream cheese

2 tbsp (28g) butter

5 tbsp (40g) confectioners' sugar, to taste

1 Oreo, crushed

1 mini Oreo, to decorate

1   Combine white chocolate chips and milk in an oversized microwave-safe mug. Microwave for about 40 seconds. Mix with a small whisk until chocolate is completely melted.

2   Add flour, baking powder, and oil and whisk until batter is smooth.

3   Add Oreos: Using a fork, smash Oreos into the batter until only small chunks of cookie remain.

4   Cook in microwave for about 1 minute. If cake is not done, heat an additional 15 seconds. Let cake cool a few minutes.

5   If desired, place the frosting ingredients in the mixing bowl of a stand mixer (or use a handheld mixer) and mix on high speed until light and fluffy. Top the cake with frosting and mini Oreo cookie. Cake is best consumed while still warm or within a few hours of being cooked.

Salted-Caramel Chocolate Cake

This recipe starts with my basic chocolate mug cake recipe and enhances it with a salted-caramel center. The melted caramel mixed with the chocolate cake adds an extra bit of bliss to each bite.

¼ cup (45g) semisweet chocolate chips

3 tbsp (45ml) fat-free milk

2 tbsp (15g) all-purpose flour

¼ tsp baking powder

½ tbsp (7.5ml) vegetable oil

2 salted caramels

TOPPING AND DECORATION, optional (serves 2)

½ cup (120ml) heavy whipping cream

2 tsp granulated sugar

caramel syrup, for drizzling

1 chopped caramel

1 Combine chocolate chips and milk in an oversized microwave-safe mug. Microwave for about 40 seconds. Mix with a small whisk until chocolate is completely melted.

2 Add flour, baking powder, and oil and whisk until batter is smooth.

3 Push the caramels into the center of the batter, until batter completely covers them.

4 Cook in microwave for about 1 minute. If cake is not done, heat an additional 15 seconds. Let cake cool a few minutes.

5 If desired, place the whipping cream and sugar in the mixing bowl of a stand mixer (or use a handheld mixer) and mix on high speed until peaks form. Top the cake with the whipped cream, drizzle with caramel syrup, and decorate with chopped caramel. Cake is best consumed while still warm.

White Chocolate Cake

Are there any white chocolate lovers out there? Well then, this cake is for you. Made with melted white chocolate, it has a pure look that reminds me of a Winter Wonderland.

¼ cup (45g) white chocolate chips

3 tbsp (45ml) whole milk

3 tbsp (22.5g) all-purpose flour

¼ tsp baking powder

½ tbsp (7.5ml) vegetable oil

CREAM CHEESE FROSTING, optional (serves 2)

2 tbsp (28g) cream cheese

2 tbsp (28g) butter

5 tbsp (40g) confectioners' sugar, to taste

1 Combine white chocolate chips and milk in an oversized microwave-safe mug. Microwave for about 40 seconds. Mix with a small whisk until chocolate is completely melted.

2 Add flour, baking powder, and oil and whisk until batter is smooth.

3 Cook in microwave for about 1 minute. If cake is not done, heat an additional 15 seconds. Let cake cool a few minutes.

4 If desired, place the frosting ingredients in the mixing bowl of a stand mixer (or use a handheld mixer) and mix on high speed until light and fluffy. Top the cake with frosting. Cake is best consumed while still warm or within a few hours of being cooked.

Triple Chocolate Cake

❧⸻❧

This cake is for the serious chocolate lover, as it is packed with three types of chocolate. There's melted dark chocolate, cocoa powder, and chocolate chips. You might need a glass of milk with this one!

1.5oz dark chocolate (1.5 squares), chopped (¼ cup)

3 tbsp (45ml) fat-free milk

2 tbsp (15g) all-purpose flour

½ tbsp (4g) unsweetened cocoa powder (Dutch-processed)

¼ tsp baking powder

1 tbsp (15ml) vegetable oil

2 tbsp (22.5g) semisweet chocolate chips

1 Combine chopped dark chocolate and milk in an oversized microwave-safe mug. Microwave for about 40 seconds. Mix with a small whisk until chocolate is completely melted.

2 Add flour, cocoa powder, baking powder, and oil and whisk until batter is smooth. Stir in chocolate chips.

3 Cook in microwave for about 1 minute. If cake is not done, heat an additional 15 seconds. Let cake cool a few minutes. Cake is best consumed while still warm or within a few hours of it being cooked.

Fruity Mug Cakes

Whether you prefer fruit-flavored desserts or you're looking for some ideas to use up leftover fruit, this is the chapter for you. Fruit is especially great to add to baked goods because it supplies a natural sweetness and brightens up desserts with vivid colors.

Creating tasty, fruit-based mug cakes was a difficult challenge when I started my mug cake adventures. Because the cake base is delicate in flavor, the use of an egg is quite noticeable, turning the batter a darker shade of yellow and giving the cake an "eggy" taste and rubbery texture. I set about trying to make my fruit-based mug cakes egg-free and as light and fluffy as possible. I hope you are as satisfied with the results as I am.

Blueberry Cake

Blueberries are wonderful to use in desserts. They look so small and innocent, but heat them up and the juicy berries burst open, adding purple and blue splashes to whatever they land on. This is a simple white cake, adorned with a sweet helping of fresh berries.

4 tbsp (30g) all-purpose flour

¼ tsp baking powder

2½ tsp granulated sugar

3 tbsp (45ml) fat-free milk

½ tbsp (7.5ml) vegetable oil

¼ tsp vanilla extract

10 blueberries

TOPPING AND DECORATION, optional (serves 2)

½ cup (120ml) heavy whipping cream

2 tsp granulated sugar

5 blueberries

confectioners' sugar, for sprinkling

1 Combine all ingredients except blueberries in an oversized microwave-safe mug. Mix with a small whisk until batter is smooth. Stir in blueberries.

2 Cook in microwave for about 1 minute. If cake is not done, heat an additional 15 seconds. Let cake cool a few minutes.

3 If desired, place the whipping cream and sugar in the mixing bowl of a stand mixer (or use a handheld mixer) and mix on high speed until peaks form. Top the cake with the whipped cream and decorate with the blueberries and a sprinkling of confectioners' sugar. Cake is best consumed while still warm or within a few hours of being cooked.

Swap It Out!
You can replace blueberries with other chopped fresh fruit like strawberries, mangoes, or peaches.

Strawberries & Cream Cake

One of my favorite summertime treats is strawberries dipped in lightly whipped sweet cream. The juicy berries not only taste succulent, they also really liven up the appearance of desserts. This recipe starts with a sweet-cream cake base and is studded with bright berries.

4 tbsp (30g) all-purpose flour

¼ tsp baking powder

1½ tbsp (19g) granulated sugar

2 tbsp (30ml) fat-free milk

2 tbsp (30g) heavy whipping cream

1 large strawberry, chopped into small pieces

TOPPING AND DECORATION, optional (serves 2)

½ cup (120ml) heavy whipping cream

2 tsp granulated sugar

1 strawberry, sliced

confectioners' sugar, for sprinkling

1 Combine all ingredients except strawberry pieces in an oversized microwave-safe mug. Mix with a small whisk until batter is smooth. Stir in strawberry chunks.

2 Cook in microwave for about 1 minute. If cake is not done, heat an additional 15 seconds. Let cake cool a few minutes.

3 If desired, place the whipping cream and sugar in the mixing bowl of stand mixer (or use a handheld mixer), and mix on high until peaks form. Top the cake with the whipped cream, a strawberry slice, and a sprinkling of confectioners' sugar. Cake is best consumed while still warm or within a few hours of being cooked.

Coconut Lover's Cake

Coconut has really grown in popularity, and now it's available in so many forms. If you adore coconut, this cake is a coconut trifecta: coconut milk, coconut flakes, and coconut water.

4 tbsp (30g) all-purpose flour

¼ tsp baking powder

2 tsp granulated sugar

2 tbsp (30ml) coconut milk

1 tbsp (15ml) coconut water

½ tbsp (7.5ml) vegetable oil

1½ tbsp (7.5g) sweetened coconut flakes

TOPPING AND DECORATION, optional (serves 2)

½ cup (120ml) heavy whipping cream

2 tsp granulated sugar

1 tbsp (5g) sweetened coconut flakes

1 Combine all ingredients except coconut flakes in an oversized microwave-safe mug. Mix with a small whisk until batter is smooth. Stir in coconut flakes.

2 Cook in microwave for about 1 minute. If cake is not done, heat an additional 15 seconds. Let cake cool a few minutes.

3 If desired, place the whipping cream and sugar in the mixing bowl of stand mixer (or use a handheld mixer) and mix on high speed until peaks form. Top the cake with the whipped cream and sprinkle the coconut flakes on top. Cake is best consumed while still warm or within a few hours of being cooked.

Apple Butter Cake

This moist and fruity cake will definitely get you in the mood for fall, thanks to the use of fresh apples and flavorful apple butter.

4 tbsp (30g) all-purpose flour

¼ tsp baking powder

2 tsp granulated sugar

2 ½ tbsp (37.5ml) fat-free milk

½ tbsp (7.5ml) vegetable oil

1 tbsp (17g) plus 1 tbsp (17g) apple butter

1 tbsp (8g) chopped apples (½-inch cubes)

1 Combine all ingredients, except chopped apples and 1 tablespoon apple butter, in an oversized microwave-safe mug. Mix with a small whisk until batter is smooth.

2 Stir in apples. Swirl in remaining apple butter with a fork.

3 Cook in microwave for about 1 minute. If cake is not done, heat an additional 15 seconds. Let cake cool a few minutes. Cake is best consumed while still warm or within a few hours of it being cooked.

Tropical Island Cake

Who doesn't fantasize about relaxing on a tropical island? I know I do. And while we can't always be doing *that*, we can still get a taste of tropical paradise with this cake, which is flavored with tropical fruits including mango, coconut, and pineapple.

4 tbsp (30g) all-purpose flour

¼ tsp baking powder

2 tsp granulated sugar

3 tbsp (45ml) coconut milk

½ tbsp (7.5ml) vegetable oil

¼ tsp vanilla extract

1 tbsp (5g) sweetened coconut flakes

1 tbsp (7g) chopped ripe mangoes

1 tbsp (13g) chopped canned pineapple (½-inch cubes)

1 Combine flour, baking powder, sugar, milk, oil, and vanilla in an oversized microwave-safe mug. Mix with a small whisk until batter is smooth. Stir in coconut flakes, mango, and pineapple.

2 Cook in microwave for about 1 minute. If cake is not done, heat an additional 15 seconds. Let cake cool a few minutes. Cake is best consumed while still warm or within a few hours of it being cooked.

A Sweet Swap
You can add or replace the chopped fruits listed with other tropical fruits like lychee, guava, and papaya.

Lemon Dream Cake

❦

This lemon cake is just dreamy. It's moist, lemony, and the perfect balance of sweet and tart. Lemon cake was my nemesis for the longest time: It was one of the most requested recipes by my readers, but I just couldn't make one that I found satisfying enough. After many trials, I finally created a lemon cake I am completely in love with, and I hope you are too.

4 tbsp (30g) all-purpose flour

¼ tsp baking powder

2 tsp granulated sugar

3 tbsp (45ml) fat-free milk

½ tbsp (7.5ml) vegetable oil

¼ tsp vanilla extract

1 tsp fresh lemon zest

1 tbsp (20g) lemon curd

TOPPING AND DECORATION, optional (serves 2)

½ cup (120ml) heavy whipping cream

2 tsp granulated sugar

½ tsp grated lemon zest

1   Combine all ingredients except lemon zest and lemon curd in an oversized microwave-safe mug. Mix with a small whisk until batter is smooth.

2   Add lemon zest and lemon curd and mix until batter is smooth.

3   Cook in microwave for about 1 minute. If cake is not done, heat an additional 15 seconds. Let cake cool a few minutes.

4   If desired, place the whipping cream and sugar in the mixing bowl of a stand mixer (or use a handheld mixer), and mix on high speed until peaks form. Top the cake with the whipped cream and lemon zest. Cake is best consumed while still warm or within a few hours of being cooked.

Pumpkin Bread Pudding Cake

Traditional bread pudding takes a lot of effort, especially to make the custard. This short-cut version takes buttery brioche bread and soaks it in a spiced pumpkin custard mix. Top with salted-caramel sauce and a scoop of ice cream for a truly indulgent dessert!

1 slice of brioche bread (about the size used for toast), untoasted, cut into ½-inch cubes

2 tbsp (30g) whisked egg (about half of 1 extra-large egg)

2 tbsp (25g) granulated sugar

2 tbsp (30ml) fat-free milk

1/16 tsp ground cinnamon

1 heaping tbsp (15g) pumpkin puree

TOPPING, optional (serves 2)

caramel sauce

ice cream

1 Arrange bread cubes in an oversized microwave-safe mug: First line the inside walls of the mug with bread cubes, then fill the middle. Stack the cubes inside the mug until you run out, so they form a tower of bread cubes.

2 In a separate mug or small bowl, whisk egg, sugar, milk, cinnamon, and pumpkin to form custard. Pour custard mixture onto bread tower, making sure the custard touches all the bread cubes.

3 Cook in microwave for about 1 minute or until custard is fully cooked. If desired, you can remove bread pudding from mug and place onto a plate. Serve warm with ice cream and caramel sauce.

Waste Not!

If you don't want to waste part of an egg, you can easily make two servings of this cake with one extra-large egg—as each serving requires half of an extra-large egg.

Skinny Mug Cakes
(Under 200 Calories!)

One of the main appeals of mug cakes is portion control. I will be the first to admit that I have no self-restraint. If I've made an entire cake, I *will* eat most of it. Which is why these single-serving cakes are perfect. I eat my cake until it's gone, but I've still only eaten one serving.

However (and here's the big BUT), just because a mug cake is one serving does not make it guilt-free. In fact, I've come across mug cake recipes that are close to a whopping 1,000 calories—yup, that's 1,000 calories for one serving! Delicious ingredients, even in small amounts, can add up quickly.

That's why I've put together the lighter recipes in this chapter, for cake lovers who want a little treat without going full-on splurge—even though there's *always* occasion for that, too! This chapter features mug cake recipes that are all under **200 calories**. These cakes might not be as rich as some of the others in this book, but they are still pretty darn gratifying, and light to boot!

Apple Spice Cake

Applesauce is a great way to keep cakes moist while reducing calorie intake. This cake uses unsweetened applesauce and fresh apple pieces to produce a tender, fall-themed cake.

APPROXIMATELY 171 CALORIES
(Without the Cream)

4 tbsp (30g) all-purpose flour

¼ tsp baking powder

2 tsp granulated sugar

1½ tbsp (22.5ml) fat-free milk

⅛ tsp ground cinnamon

2 tbsp (30g) unsweetened applesauce

2 tbsp (16g) chopped apples (½-inch cubes)

TOPPING AND DECORATION,
optional (serves 2)

½ cup (120ml) heavy whipping cream

2 tsp granulated sugar

1 tsp ground cinnamon

1   Combine all ingredients except apple cubes in an oversized microwave-safe mug. Mix with a small whisk until batter is smooth. Stir in apple cubes.

2   Cook in microwave for about 1 minute. If cake is not done, heat an additional 15 seconds. Let cake cool a few minutes.

3   If desired, place the whipping cream and sugar in the mixing bowl of a stand mixer (or use a handheld mixer), and mix on high speed until peaks form. Top the cake with the whipped cream and sift a little cinnamon powder on top of the cake. Cake is best consumed warm or within a few hours of being cooked.

Skinny Tip

I made fresh whipped cream for this photo, but the cake tastes delicious without the cream. You could also add a dollop of light Cool Whip for only 25 extra calories.

Banana Cake

Classic banana bread is such a comforting treat, but the calorie count is killer. This skinnied-up version still satisfies the cravings, without calling for a long session at the gym afterward.

Note: Make sure you scoop up 2 tablespoons of already-mashed banana, which is more than 2 tablespoons of unmashed banana cut from the fruit. The more overripe the banana, the easier it will be to whisk. Also, stay away from frozen bananas as they retain a great amount of water even after they are defrosted that will make the cake gummy.

APPROXIMATELY
200 CALORIES

4 tbsp (30g) all-purpose
  flour
½ tsp baking powder
2 tsp granulated sugar
3 tbsp (45ml) fat-free milk
⅛ tsp ground cinnamon
2 tbsp (30g) mashed
  overripe banana (about
  half of a large banana)

TOPPING AND
DECORATION, optional
1 tsp confectioners' sugar
1 banana chip

1 Combine all ingredients in an oversized microwave-safe mug. Mix with a small whisk until batter is smooth.

2 Cook in microwave for about 1 minute. If cake is not done, heat an additional 15 seconds. Let cake cool a few minutes.

3 If desired, sift the confectioners' sugar on top of the cake and insert a banana chip for decoration. Cake is best consumed while still warm or within a few hours of being cooked.

Cinnamon Cake

This simple cinnamon-infused cake is light and fluffy and low in calories. What more could you ask for in a cake?

APPROXIMATELY
181 CALORIES

4 tbsp (30g) all-purpose
    flour
¼ tsp baking powder
3 tsp granulated sugar
3 tbsp (45ml) fat-free
    milk
½ tbsp (7.5g) plain
    non-fat Greek yogurt
⅛ tsp ground cinnamon

1. Combine all ingredients in an oversized microwave-safe mug. Mix with a small whisk until batter is smooth.

2. Cook in microwave for about 1 minute. If cake is not done, heat an additional 15 seconds. Let cake cool a few minutes. Cake is best consumed while still warm or within a few hours of it being cooked.

Pumpkin Lite Cake

~ ❦ ~

Here is a lighter version of the Pumpkin Spice Cake on page 139. You'll get the same warm autumn glow after tasting this reduced-calorie cake, which is spiced with cinnamon.

APPROXIMATELY
190 CALORIES

4 tbsp (30g) all-purpose
  flour
¼ tsp baking powder
1 tbsp (12.5g)
  granulated sugar
2½ tbsp (37.5ml) fat-
  free milk
2 tbsp (30g) canned
  pumpkin puree
⅛ tsp ground cinnamon

1 Combine all ingredients in an oversized microwave-safe mug. Mix with a small whisk until batter is smooth.

2 Cook in microwave for about 1 minute. If cake is not done, heat an additional 15 seconds. Let cake cool a few minutes. Cake is best consumed while still warm or within a few hours of it being cooked.

Chocolate Ice Cream Cake

Would you believe me if I told you that you can make a delectable chocolate cake with only three ingredients, and the main ingredient is chocolate ice cream? *And* it's under 200 calories? Yes, such a magical dessert does exist!

Note #1: You must use a super-premium, **full-fat ice cream** *(yep, I said full-fat!). I like using Häagen-Dazs. There is no other source of fat in the ingredients, so low-fat or fat-free ice creams won't cut it.*

Note #2: You must use **cake flour** *to get the right texture. Otherwise, it will have a much rougher texture and will not taste like a cake.*

APPROXIMATELY 180 CALORIES

4 tbsp (50g) super-premium chocolate ice cream with chocolate chips (*not* low-fat or fat-free)

2 tbsp (12.5g) cake flour (*not* all-purpose)

⅛ tsp baking powder

1 Melt ice cream in an oversized microwave-safe mug for about 20 seconds.

2 Add cake flour and baking powder. Mix with a small whisk until batter is smooth.

3 Cook in microwave for about 1 minute. If cake is not done, heat an additional 15 seconds. Let cake cool a few minutes. Cake is best consumed while still warm or within a few hours of it being cooked.

Blueberry Delight Cake

The classic blueberry cake is lightened up with some plain Greek yogurt, a magical ingredient that can make almost any dish healthier without affecting the taste. Moist and bursting with sweet berries, this cake is so scrumptious you won't be able to tell it's less than 200 calories.

APPROXIMATELY
196 CALORIES

4 tbsp (30g) all-purpose flour

¼ tsp baking powder

3 tsp granulated sugar

3 tbsp (45ml) fat-free milk

½ tbsp (7.5g) plain non-fat Greek yogurt

¼ tsp vanilla extract

8 blueberries

1 Combine all ingredients except blueberries in an oversized microwave-safe mug. Mix with a small whisk until batter is smooth. Stir in blueberries.

2 Cook in microwave for about 1 minute. If cake is not done, heat an additional 15 seconds. Let cake cool a few minutes. Cake is best consumed while still warm or within a few hours of it being cooked.

Strawberry Yogurt Cake

This cake is flavored with strawberry yogurt, adding a little tanginess to each bite. You can substitute other fruit flavors if you like.

APPROXIMATELY
199 CALORIES

4 tbsp (30g) all-purpose flour

¼ tsp baking powder

3 tsp granulated sugar

2 tbsp (30ml) fat-free milk

2 tbsp (30g) non-fat strawberry Greek yogurt

1 Combine all ingredients in an oversized microwave-safe mug. Mix with a small whisk until batter is smooth.

2 Cook in microwave for about 1 minute. If cake is not done, heat an additional 15 seconds. Let cake cool a few minutes. Cake is best consumed while still warm or within a few hours of it being cooked.

4-Ingredients-or-Less Mug Cakes

Most mug cakes in this book take only five minutes to make, but if that's not motivation enough to get you started, this chapter makes things *even easier.* Do you shy away from recipes with long lists of ingredients? Problem solved! These recipes are the ultimate no-fuss desserts: They're ready in five minutes **and** they use only four ingredients or less. Say goodbye to lengthy shopping lists and get in the kitchen to make your cake and eat it, too! (You can thank me later.)

2-Ingredient Flourless Nutella Cake

This is by far the easiest recipe in the book and my proudest creation. Some history: Two years ago, I created a recipe for a 2-Ingredient Flourless Nutella Cake. The original version makes a full cake and is baked. When I posted it on my blog, *Kirbie's Cravings*, I experienced for the first time what it was like to have a recipe go viral on the Internet. I've adapted that recipe here for an even easier Nutella mug cake, and the results are just as rich and delicious as the original.

Note: While most desserts taste best warm and straight out of the oven, this is one recipe where you must give the cake several hours to settle so that the flavors can fully develop. If you try to eat the cake right away, it will likely taste a little eggy. Just give it a few hours (I know it's hard, but trust me, it's worth it!) and you'll be enjoying a heavenly, rich, flourless Nutella cake that rivals the real thing.

1 large egg
¼ cup (74g) Nutella

TOPPING AND DECORATION, optional (serves 2)
2oz dark chocolate, chopped
¼ cup (60ml) heavy cream
chopped walnuts, for sprinkling

1 For the cake, break egg into an oversized microwave-safe mug and whisk.

2 Add Nutella and whisk vigorously until the batter is smooth and the egg is fully incorporated. Because the mixture is so dark, it will be hard to see if egg streaks remain. Lift your whisk a couple times to make sure you don't see evidence of unmixed egg still in the batter.

3 Cook in microwave for about 1 minute. Cake will look the slightest bit gooey on top, but as long as the cake has risen and is set, it should be ready. Let cake sit for several hours before eating, so the chocolate hazelnut flavor can fully develop and overcome any eggy taste.

4 For the frosting if desired, put the chopped chocolate into a bowl. Then heat the heavy cream in a small pot. Once it begins to boil, remove from the stove, and pour the heavy cream into the bowl with the chocolate. Stir and mix until the chocolate is completely melted. Let the ganache cool (you can speed this up by putting it in the fridge for 45 minutes). You may need to stir it again to make it smooth and shiny.

5 Once the ganache is cooled and set, put it in a piping bag and frost the cake. Sprinkle with chopped walnuts. Cake is best consumed within a few hours of being cooked.

4-Ingredient Nutella Cake

If you read my blog, *Kirbie's Cravings*, you know I have a serious Nutella obsession. (We're talking 100-plus Nutella recipes that I have tested, tasted, and then tested and tasted again.) Luckily, others seem to share my passion: This 4-Ingredient Nutella Cake is the most popular mug cake on the site. I've eliminated all non-essential ingredients, allowing Nutella to really be the star. The cake is incredibly moist, rich, and the perfect treat for Nutella fans. You won't believe it's only four ingredients.

4 tbsp (30g) all-purpose flour

¼ tsp baking powder

3 tbsp (45ml) fat-free milk

¼ cup (74g) Nutella

1 Combine all ingredients in an oversized microwave-safe mug. Mix with a small whisk until batter is smooth.

2 Cook in microwave for about 1 minute. If cake is not done, heat an additional 15 seconds. Let cake cool a few minutes. Cake is best consumed while still warm or within a few hours of it being cooked.

Chocolate Quartet Cake

Yes, you can make chocolate cake with only four ingredients! The texture is not quite as moist as the other chocolate cakes in this book, but it's absolutely delicious with a cup of coffee.

Note: For best results, eat this cake right away. The cake has a lower fat content because no oil is added. As a result, it tends to dry out if left out for several hours.

¼ cup (45g) semisweet chocolate chips

3 tbsp (45ml) plus 1 tbsp (15ml) whole milk

3 tbsp (22.5g) all-purpose flour

¼ tsp baking powder

1 Combine chocolate chips and 3 tablespoons milk (reserving 1 tablespoon) in an oversized microwave-safe mug. Microwave for about 40 seconds. Mix with a small whisk until chocolate is completely melted.

2 Add flour and baking powder and whisk until batter is smooth.

3 Add remaining 1 tablespoon milk and whisk.

4 Cook in microwave for about 1 minute. If cake is not done, heat an additional 15 seconds. Let cake cool a few minutes. Cake is best consumed while still warm.

Chocolate Bread Cake

This moist chocolaty quick-bread cake uses just three ingredients! All you need is flour, baking powder, and some chocolate ice cream. Just make sure you use a super-premium, full-fat ice cream (like Häagen-Dazs), otherwise this cake won't work.

4 tbsp (50g) super-premium chocolate ice cream (*not* low-fat or fat-free)

2 tbsp (15g) all-purpose flour

¼ tsp baking powder

TOPPING AND DECORATION, *optional (serves 2)*

½ cup (120ml) heavy whipping cream

2 tsp granulated sugar

10 raspberries

1 Melt ice cream in an oversized microwave-safe mug for about 20 seconds.

2 Add flour and baking powder. Mix with a small whisk until batter is smooth.

3 Cook in microwave for about 1 minute. If cake is not done, heat an additional 15 seconds. Let cake cool a few minutes.

4 If desired, place the whipping cream and sugar in the mixing bowl of stand mixer (or use a handheld mixer), and mix on high speed until peaks form. Top the cake with the whipped cream and decorate with the raspberries. Cake is best consumed while still warm.

Ice Cream Options

Create your own variations with different ice-cream flavors. Just make sure you choose strong flavors like espresso, chocolate, and caramel.

Andes Mints Cake

The popular after-dinner mints are melted down to provide a soothing, mint-chocolate cake. Each bite provides a cooling sensation that your mouth and stomach will welcome.

8 Andes Mints, broken in half

3 tbsp (45ml) whole milk

3 tbsp (22.5g) all-purpose flour

¼ tsp baking powder

1 Combine chocolate mints and milk in an oversized microwave-safe mug. Microwave for about 40 seconds. Mix with a small whisk until chocolate is completely melted.

2 Add remaining ingredients and whisk until batter is smooth.

3 Cook in microwave for about 1 minute. If cake is not done, heat an additional 15 seconds. Let cake cool a few minutes. Cake is best consumed while still warm.

Breakfast Mug Cakes

Are you a breakfast lover? If so, you're in for a sweet treat with the recipes in this chapter, as they feature delectable breakfast favorites in mug cake form—from Blueberry Muffin Streusel to Maple Syrup Pancake to French Toast. As always, these tasty mug cakes take only five minutes or less to prepare, a bonus for those of us who need our breakfast on-the-go. But don't let the time of day dictate your mug cake cravings: Breakfast can happen anywhere, at any time. Especially when it's this delicious.

Blueberry Muffin Streusel Cake

I am a strong believer that streusel makes everything taste better. This muffin cake is studded with blueberries and then covered with a generous amount of streusel. The cake takes a little more effort if you want to add the topping, but streusel is always worth it, at least in my book! Because this is a muffin cake, expect the crumb to be a little tighter than in the Blueberry Cake on page 16.

MUFFIN

4 tbsp (30g) all-purpose flour

⅛ tsp baking powder

1/16 tsp baking soda

2 tsp granulated sugar

3 tbsp (45ml) fat-free milk

½ tbsp (7.5ml) vegetable oil

8 fresh blueberries

STREUSEL TOPPING
(serves 2)

½ tbsp (7g) cold butter, chopped into tiny pieces

¾ tbsp (5.6g) all-purpose flour

1 tbsp (12.5g) plus 1 tsp (4g) light brown sugar

1/16 tsp ground cinnamon

1 For the Muffin: Combine all muffin ingredients except blueberries in an oversized microwave-safe mug. Mix with a small whisk until batter is smooth. Stir in blueberries.

2 For the Streusel Topping: In a separate small bowl, mix streusel ingredients until butter pieces are completely coated in the flour, sugar, and cinnamon.

3 Sprinkle crumbles of streusel on top of muffin batter, spreading out evenly across surface of batter.

4 Cook in microwave for about 1 minute. If cake is not done, heat an additional 15 seconds. Let cake cool a few minutes. Cake is best consumed while still warm or within a few hours of it being cooked.

Skip a Step!
If you don't care for streusel, you can just exclude it and save some time. Or you can sprinkle coarse sugar on top as an alternative.

Coffee Cake

This sour cream-based cake has tangy undertones and is covered with a buttery cinnamon streusel topping.

CAKE

4 tbsp (30g) all-purpose flour

¼ tsp baking powder

3 tsp granulated sugar

2 tbsp (30ml) fat-free milk

½ tbsp (7.5ml) vegetable oil

2 tbsp (30g) sour cream

STREUSEL TOPPING
(serves 2)

½ tbsp (7g) cold butter, chopped into tiny pieces

¾ tbsp (5.6g) all-purpose flour

1 tbsp (12.5g) plus 1 tsp (4g) light brown sugar

$\frac{1}{16}$ tsp ground cinnamon

1 For the Cake: Combine all cake ingredients in an oversized microwave-safe mug. Mix with a small whisk until batter is smooth.

2 For the Streusel Topping: In a separate small bowl, mix streusel ingredients until butter pieces are completely coated in the flour, sugar, and cinnamon.

3 Sprinkle crumbles of streusel on top of cake batter, spreading out evenly across surface of batter.

4 Cook in microwave for about 1 minute. If cake is not done, heat an additional 15 seconds. Let cake cool a few minutes. Cake is best consumed while still warm or within a few hours of it being cooked.

French Toast Cake

Breakfast just got a whole lot simpler with this easy French toast mug cake recipe. It's also a good use of day-old bread.

1 slice of bread (either white or brown), untoasted, cut into ½-inch cubes

2 tbsp (30g) whisked egg (about half of 1 extra-large egg)

2 tbsp (30ml) fat-free milk

⅛ tsp ground cinnamon

1 tbsp (12.5g) granulated sugar

maple syrup (for serving)

1 Arrange bread cubes in an oversized microwave-safe mug: First line the inside walls of the mug with bread cubes, then fill the middle. Stack the cubes inside the mug until you run out, so they form a tower of bread cubes.

2 In a separate mug or small bowl, mix egg, milk, cinnamon, and sugar with a small whisk. Pour mixture onto bread tower, making sure the batter touches all the bread cubes.

3 Cook in microwave for about 1 minute or until egg-custard mixture is completely cooked. You can eat straight from the mug or easily transfer the tower of French toast onto a plate. Serve with syrup.

Waste Not!

If you don't want to waste part of an egg, you can easily make two servings of this cake with one extra-large egg—as each serving requires half of an extra-large egg.

Honey Swirl Cake

Honey cake is so simple and so charming in its simplicity. The taste of honey always brings a smile to my lips. I enjoy eating this cake over a leisurely weekend breakfast with a cup of steaming-hot tea.

4 tbsp (30g) all-purpose flour

¼ tsp baking powder

3 tsp granulated sugar

3 tbsp (45ml) fat-free milk

½ tbsp (7.5ml) vegetable oil

1 tbsp (21g) plus ½ tbsp (11g) honey

1 Combine all ingredients except ½ tablespoon honey in an oversized microwave-safe mug. Mix with a small whisk until batter is smooth.

2 Swirl in remaining honey with a fork. Be careful not to completely mix it into the batter, as you want to leave swirls of honey in your cake.

3 Cook in microwave for about 1 minute. If cake is not done, heat an additional 15 seconds. Let cake cool a few minutes. Cake is best consumed while still warm or within a few hours of it being cooked.

Espresso Cake

If your morning usually includes a cup of coffee, why not add it directly into your breakfast? Many baked goods contain espresso powder to deepen the flavor, but this one lets the coffee be the star.

4 tbsp (30g) all-purpose flour

¼ tsp baking powder

3 tsp granulated sugar

3 tbsp (45ml) fat-free milk

½ tbsp (7.5ml) vegetable oil

½ tsp espresso powder

½ tsp confectioners' sugar, optional

1 Combine all ingredients add, except the confectioners' sugar in an oversized microwave-safe mug. Mix with a small whisk until batter is smooth.

2 Cook in microwave for about 1 minute. If cake is not done, heat an additional 15 seconds. Let cake cool for a few minutes, and then, if desired, sift a little confectioners' sugar on top of the cake. Cake is best consumed while still warm or within a few hours of it being cooked.

Maple Syrup Pancake

My ideal breakfast almost always involves pancakes. With this recipe, you can make just a single pancake. No need to whip up a family-sized amount of batter or flip the pancakes on the griddle. Just mix, microwave, drizzle some syrup, and enjoy!

¼ cup (30g) pancake mix (like Bisquick)

2 tbsp (30ml) fat-free milk

1 tbsp (20g) maple syrup, plus additional for drizzling

TOPPING AND DECORATION, optional (serves 2)

½ cup (120ml) heavy whipping cream

2 tsp granulated sugar

mini pancakes

1 Combine all ingredients in an oversized microwave-safe mug. Mix with a small whisk until ingredients are combined and only small lumps remain.

2 Cook in microwave for about 1 minute. If cake is not done, heat an additional 15 seconds. Let cake cool a few minutes.

3 Place the whipping cream and sugar in the mixing bowl of stand mixer (or use a handheld mixer), and mix on high speed until peaks form. Top the cake with the whipped cream and mini pancakes, and drizzle with syrup, if desired.

Banana Bread Cake

If you've ever made banana bread, you know that mixing the ingredients together is a cinch. The problem is the long wait after as your bread bakes. Enter: instant banana bread! In just five minutes, you can have a fresh-"baked" banana bread mug cake, perfect for breakfast or any other time of day.

Note: Make sure you scoop up 2 tablespoons of already-mashed banana, which is more than 2 tablespoons of unmashed banana cut from the fruit. The more overripe the banana, the easier it will be to whisk. Also, stay away from frozen bananas as they retain a great amount of water even after they are defrosted that will make the cake gummy.

4 tbsp (30g) all-purpose flour

½ tsp baking powder

2 tsp granulated sugar

2½ tbsp (37.5ml) fat-free milk

½ tbsp (7.5ml) vegetable oil

⅛ tsp ground cinnamon

2 tbsp (30g) mashed overripe banana (about half of a large banana)

1 tbsp (8g) chopped pecans or walnuts (optional)

1 Combine all ingredients except nuts in an oversized microwave-safe mug. Mix with a small whisk until batter is smooth. Stir in pecans or walnuts.

2 Cook in microwave for about 1 minute. If cake is not done, heat an additional 15 seconds. Let cake cool a few minutes. Cake is best consumed while still warm or within a few hours of it being cooked.

Coffee and Tea Mug Cakes

What's better than a cup of crisp, flavorful coffee or delicately fragrant tea? Pastries, of course! Specifically, pastries flavored with those beloved beverages. Whether you're a coffee addict or tea connoisseur, this chapter has you covered—now you can get your favorite caffeine fix in edible form! I consume both beverages on a daily basis and the only thing I love more than drinking them is eating sweets flavored with them. These coffee and tea mug cakes are good to the last drop—errrr, bite!

Gingerbread-Spice Latte Cake

Add a little spice to your day with this scrumptious winter-season snack. The popular holiday drink is turned into cake form, with hints of molasses, ginger, and espresso.

4 tbsp (30g) all-purpose flour

¼ tsp baking powder

3 tbsp (45ml) fat-free milk

½ tbsp (7.5ml) vegetable oil

1 tbsp (21g) dark molasses

1 tbsp (12.5g) dark brown sugar

¼ tsp espresso powder

½ tsp ground ginger

1/16 tsp ground cinnamon

1 Combine all ingredients in an oversized microwave-safe mug. Mix with a small whisk until batter is smooth.

2 Cook in microwave for about 1 minute. If cake is not done, heat an additional 15 seconds. Let cake cool a few minutes. Cake is best consumed while still warm or within a few hours of it being cooked.

Java Chip Cake

❦

Much like the popular Starbucks' drink, this is an espresso-flavored cake studded with bittersweet chocolate chips. The coffee and dark chocolate pairing is absolutely dreamy. I like to top mine off with whipped cream, just like at the coffee shop.

- 4 tbsp (30g) all-purpose flour
- ¼ tsp baking powder
- 1 tbsp (12.5g) granulated sugar
- 3 tbsp (45ml) fat-free milk
- ½ tbsp (7.5ml) vegetable oil
- ½ tsp espresso powder
- 1 heaping tbsp (11g) mini bittersweet chocolate chips

1 Combine all ingredients except chocolate chips in an oversized microwave-safe mug. Mix with a small whisk until batter is smooth. Stir in chocolate chips.

2 Cook in microwave for about 1 minute. If cake is not done, heat an additional 15 seconds. Let cake cool a few minutes. Cake is best consumed while still warm or within a few hours of it being cooked.

Matcha Green Tea Cake

Matcha is a green tea powder that brings a natural, vibrant green hue to this cake. The unique and complex flavor of matcha truly comes through, and it has a lot of health benefits as well, which is a great justification for eating this yummy mug cake!

Note: Use premium-grade matcha powder meant for tea ceremonies and not the culinary-grade version. If you compare them side by side, you'll immediately see the difference in color: The lower-quality matcha powders will turn the cake more of a yellowish green. My favorite brand is Maeda-En, the gold canister quality.

4 tbsp (30g) all-purpose flour

1 tsp premium matcha powder

¼ tsp baking powder

1 tbsp (12.5g) granulated sugar

3 tbsp (45ml) fat-free milk

½ tbsp (7.5ml) vegetable oil

1 Combine flour, matcha, and baking powder in an oversized microwave-safe mug. Whisk together until matcha powder is fully incorporated into the flour.

2 Add remaining ingredients and mix with a small whisk until batter is smooth and no matcha powder clumps remain (a few dark green specks are okay, but you don't want any lumps).

3 Cook in microwave for about 1 minute. If cake is not done, heat an additional 15 seconds. Let cake cool a few minutes. Cake is best consumed while still warm or within a few hours of it being cooked.

Mocha Cake

A little bit of chocolate makes everything taste better, which is probably why mocha is such a popular coffee beverage. This cake is made with espresso powder and just a touch of cocoa.

3 tbsp (22.5g) all-purpose flour

¼ tsp baking powder

2 tbsp (25g) granulated sugar

3 tbsp (45ml) fat-free milk

½ tbsp (7.5ml) vegetable oil

1 tbsp (7.5g) unsweetened cocoa powder (Dutch-processed)

1 tsp espresso powder

1 Combine all ingredients in an oversized microwave-safe mug. Mix with a small whisk until batter is smooth.

2 Cook in microwave for about 1 minute. If cake is not done, heat an additional 15 seconds. Let cake cool a few minutes. Cake is best consumed while still warm or within a few hours of it being cooked.

Pumpkin-Spice Latte Cake

A touch of pumpkin, a dash of spice, a shot of espresso, and a generous pour of creamy milk—that's why the pumpkin-spice latte is my quintessential fall beverage. As soon as the leaves start changing color and the briskness creeps into the air, I start craving these oh-so-satisfying coffee treats. I've learned to make my own so I don't spend too much money buying them; and, naturally, I've created a Pumpkin-Spice Latte Cake, which is just as pleasurable as the drink.

4 tbsp (30g) all-purpose flour

¼ tsp baking powder

2 tbsp (25g) granulated sugar

2 tbsp (30ml) fat-free milk

½ tbsp (7.5ml) vegetable oil

½ tsp pumpkin spice

¼ tsp espresso powder

2 tbsp (30g) canned pumpkin puree

1 Combine all ingredients in an oversized microwave-safe mug. Mix with a small whisk until batter is smooth.

2 Cook in microwave for about 1 minute 30 seconds. If cake is not done, heat an additional 15 seconds. Let cake cool a few minutes. Cake is best consumed while still warm or within a few hours of it being cooked.

Thai Tea Cake

Thai iced tea is one of my favorite beverages, with its fiery orange color and fragrant flavor. This scrumptious cake produces the same brilliant shade of orange.

4 tbsp (30g) all-purpose flour

¼ tsp baking powder

3 tsp granulated sugar

3 tbsp (45ml) fat-free milk

½ tbsp (7.5ml) vegetable oil

1 tbsp (14g) instant Thai tea mix (with sugar and cream in the powder)

1 Combine all ingredients in an oversized microwave-safe mug. Mix with a small whisk until batter is smooth.

2 Cook in microwave for about 1 minute. If cake is not done, heat an additional 15 seconds. Let cake cool a few minutes. Cake is best consumed while still warm or within a few hours of it being cooked.

Where Can I Find It?
Instant Thai tea mix packages can be purchased at most Asian grocery stores.

Vanilla Latte Cake

Sometimes, simple is best. Vanilla-flavored lattes may sound boring with so many other options out there, but this cake is no wallflower. It's enhanced with vanilla bean paste, giving it a wonderfully aromatic finish.

4 tbsp (30g) all-purpose flour

¼ tsp baking powder

1 tbsp (12.5g) granulated sugar

3 tbsp (45ml) fat-free milk

½ tbsp (7.5ml) vegetable oil

¼ tsp espresso powder

½ tsp vanilla bean paste

1 Combine all ingredients in an oversized microwave-safe mug. Mix with a small whisk until batter is smooth.

2 Cook in microwave for about 1 minute. If cake is not done, heat an additional 15 seconds. Let cake cool a few minutes. Cake is best consumed while still warm or within a few hours of it being cooked.

Nostalgic Mug Cakes

It seems the older we get, the more we look back fondly on our childhood. This section is a trip down memory lane, offering up confections you were likely first introduced to as a child—from s'mores to Jell-O to the much-loved Hostess cupcakes.

While we can't travel back in time, we can relive some precious moments through these cakes. And of course, these recipes are also great to make and share with any kids in your life.

Funfetti Cake

Funfetti cake was always my choice for a birthday cake when I was growing up. Colorful sprinkles melted into a simple white cake make this a festive party recipe for big kids and small kids alike. It's fun to look at and, of course, to *eat*.

4 tbsp (30g) all-purpose flour

¼ tsp baking powder

2 tsp granulated sugar

3 tbsp (45ml) fat-free milk

½ tbsp (7.5ml) vegetable oil

¼ tsp vanilla extract

½ tbsp (6g) rainbow sprinkles

TOPPING AND DECORATION, *optional*

vanilla ice cream

rainbow sprinkles, for sprinkling

1 Combine all ingredients except sprinkles in an oversized microwave-safe mug. Mix with a small whisk until batter is smooth. Stir in the sprinkles.

2 Cook in microwave for about 1 minute. If cake is not done, heat an additional 15 seconds. Let cake cool a few minutes.

3 If desired, top the cake with a scoop of vanilla ice cream and rainbow sprinkles. Cake is best consumed while still warm or within a few hours of being cooked.

Hostess (Cup)cake

The flavors of a Hostess cupcake are mimicked in this chocolate cake base and fluffy melted marshmallow creme center.

3 tbsp (22.5g) all-purpose flour

¼ tsp baking powder

1 tbsp (12.5g) granulated sugar

3 tbsp (45ml) fat-free milk

½ tbsp (7.5ml) vegetable oil

1 tbsp (7.5g) unsweetened cocoa powder (Dutch-processed)

1 tbsp (6g) marshmallow creme (like Jet-Puffed or Fluff)

TOPPING (serves 2)

2 tbsp (22g) dark chocolate chips

4 tbsp (55g) white buttercream frosting, store-bought

1 Combine all ingredients except marshmallow creme in an oversized microwave-safe mug. Mix with a small whisk until batter is smooth.

2 Scoop out ¼ cup of batter and set aside. Only a thin layer of batter should remain at the bottom of the mug.

3 Add marshmallow creme to the mug. Your creme must be as close to the bottom of the batter as possible, so it won't float to the top during cooking.

4 Return the scooped-out batter back into the mug on top of the marshmallow creme, making sure to cover it entirely. The weight of the batter will help keep the creme inside the cake during cooking.

5 Cook in microwave for about 1 minute. If cake is not done, heat an additional 15 seconds. Let cake cool a few minutes.

6 For the frosting, melt the chocolate chips and pour over the cake. Place the cake in the fridge to harden the chocolate on top. Place the buttercream frosting in a piping bag, and then add the decorative swirls to the top of the cake. Cake is best consumed within a few hours of being cooked.

Jell-O Cake

This colorful cake tastes just like the gelatin dessert. You can experiment with all sorts of flavors and colors. (Note: Kids will love this one, too!)

4 tbsp (30g) all-purpose flour

¼ tsp baking powder

1 tsp granulated sugar

3 tbsp (45ml) fat-free milk

½ tbsp (7.5ml) vegetable oil

1 tbsp (14g) Jell-O gelatin powder (any flavor you like, but *not* sugar-free)

TOPPING AND DECORATION, optional (serves 2)

½ cup (120ml) heavy whipping cream

2 tsp granulated sugar

rainbow sprinkles

1 Combine all ingredients in an oversized microwave-safe mug. Mix with a small whisk until batter is smooth.

2 Cook in microwave for about 1 minute. If cake is not done, heat an additional 15 seconds. Let cake cool a few minutes.

3 If desired, place the whipping cream and sugar in the mixing bowl of a stand mixer (or use a handheld mixer), and mix on high speed until peaks form. Top the cake with the whipped cream and decorate with rainbow sprinkles. Cake is best consumed while still warm or within a few hours of being cooked.

Hot Cocoa Cake

I always crave hot chocolate during the winter months. It's so delicious and warming and comforting—there's nothing quite like it. Growing up, my mom would make me hot chocolate for breakfast on school days when it was especially chilly outside. This mug cake is flavored with hot cocoa mix and mini marshmallows, just like the hot chocolate from my childhood.

3 tbsp (22.5g) all-purpose flour

¼ tsp baking powder

2 tsp granulated sugar

3 tbsp (45ml) fat-free milk

½ tbsp (7.5ml) vegetable oil

1 tbsp (14g) hot cocoa mix

5 mini marshmallows

1 Combine all ingredients except marshmallows in an oversized microwave-safe mug. Mix with a small whisk until batter is smooth. Sprinkle mini marshmallows on top of the batter.

2 Cook in microwave for about 1 minute. If cake is not done, heat an additional 15 seconds. Let cake cool a few minutes. Cake is best consumed while still warm or within a few hours of it being cooked.

Pudding Cake

A few years ago, cake-mix brands began adding a cup of pudding mix to their cake-mix batter. The pudding makes cakes extra moist, so I've used that trick for this yummy mug cake recipe too. Just one scoop of the magic ingredient makes for an especially pleasurable experience.

Note: Simply add the pudding mix powder as is. Do not make the mix into a pudding first.

3 tbsp (22.5g) all-purpose flour

¼ tsp baking powder

2 tsp granulated sugar

3 tbsp (45ml) fat-free milk

½ tbsp (7.5ml) vegetable oil

1 tbsp (14g) instant vanilla pudding mix (or any flavor you like)

1   Combine all ingredients in an oversized microwave-safe mug. Mix with a small whisk until batter is smooth.

2   Cook in microwave for about 1 minute. If cake is not done, heat an additional 15 seconds. Let cake cool a few minutes. Cake is best consumed while still warm or within a few hours of it being cooked.

Mix & Match
I usually stick with vanilla pudding mix, but you can mix and match flavors to change the flavor of the cake.

Peanut Butter & Jelly Cake

I remember eating peanut butter and jelly sandwiches constantly as a kid, but I rarely eat them as an adult. So, peanut butter and jelly-flavored desserts? Sign me up!

This cake starts with a peanut butter cake base while the inside is filled with a jam or jelly surprise. I prefer jam because of its thicker consistency. Don't worry if your jam bubbles to the surface when the cake is cooking; it creates a nice lava effect.

4 tbsp (30g) all-purpose flour

¼ tsp baking powder

4 tsp granulated sugar

4 tbsp (60ml) fat-free milk

3 tbsp (48g) peanut butter (store-bought)

1 heaping tbsp (20g) jam

1 Combine all ingredients except jam in an oversized microwave-safe mug. Mix with a small whisk until batter is smooth.

2 Using an ice-cream scoop, scoop out about half of the batter and set aside.

3 Drop tablespoon of jam into the center of the batter in the mug, and then return the scooped-out batter back into the mug, covering the jam completely.

4 Cook in microwave for about 1 minute. If cake is not done, heat an additional 15 seconds. Let cake cool a few minutes. Cake is best consumed while still warm or within a few hours of it being cooked.

Peanut Butter Cup Cake

Growing up, my favorite Halloween candy was peanut butter cups. I still haven't really outgrown them. This cake replicates the coveted candy by sandwiching creamy peanut butter in the middle of a chocolate cake.

3 tbsp (22.5g) all-purpose flour

¼ tsp baking powder

1 tbsp (12.5g) granulated sugar

3 tbsp (45ml) fat-free milk

½ tbsp (7.5ml) vegetable oil

1 tbsp (7.5g) unsweetened cocoa powder (Dutch-processed)

1 tbsp (16g) creamy peanut butter (store-bought)

CHOCOLATE GANACHE FROSTING, optional
(serves 2)

2oz dark chocolate, chopped

¼ cup (60ml) heavy cream

chocolate sprinkles

1 For the cake, combine all ingredients except peanut butter in an oversized microwave-safe mug. Mix with a small whisk until batter is smooth.

2 Gently place peanut butter in the middle of the batter and press down lightly on the spread until the cake batter just barely covers the peanut butter. The peanut butter will sink down during cooking, so you don't want to push down too far or it will end up at the bottom.

3 Cook in microwave for about 1 minute. If cake is not done, heat an additional 15 seconds. Let cake cool a few minutes.

4 For the frosting if desired, put the chopped dark chocolate in a small bowl. Then heat the heavy cream in a small pot. Once it begins to boil, remove from the stove. Pour the heavy cream over the chopped chocolate, and stir and mix until the chocolate is completely melted. Let the ganache cool and set (you can speed up this process by putting it in the fridge for about 45 minutes). You may need to stir it again to make it smooth and shiny.

5 Once the ganache is cooled, put it in a piping bag and frost the cake. Decorate with chocolate sprinkles. Cake is best consumed with a few hours of being cooked.

S'Mores Cake

Ah, s'mores. The ultimate childhood snack experience. My favorite part of a s'more is the roasted marshmallow: I love the way it puffs up and develops a thin crispy skin around that gooey melty center. Eating too many regular marshmallows usually leaves me feeling a little sick to my stomach. But when the marshmallows are roasted, they are transformed in flavor and texture and I feel like I can eat them forever.

This recipe requires extra equipment if you want to achieve the roasted-marshmallow effect. Unfortunately, a microwave can't give marshmallows that beautiful golden-brown tinge. Instead, you'll need either a kitchen torch or an oven to get the roasted look and texture. But if you love s'mores, it's worth the little bit of work.

4 tbsp (24g) ground
   graham cracker crumbs
   (about 1 sheet of
   graham crackers)

1 tbsp (14g) melted butter

¼ cup (45g) semisweet
   chocolate chips

3 tbsp (45ml) fat-free milk

2 tbsp (15g) all-purpose flour

¼ tsp baking powder

½ tbsp (7.5ml) vegetable oil

18–20 mini marshmallows

chocolate star, optional
   for decoration

1 Combine graham cracker crumbs and melted butter in an oversized microwave-safe mug. Mix together until butter completely coats all the crumbs. Press down to form a crust evenly across the bottom of the mug.

2 Place chocolate and milk in a separate small bowl. Microwave for 40 seconds and mix with a small whisk until chocolate is completely melted.

3 Add flour, baking powder, and oil and mix with a small whisk until batter is smooth. Pour into mug, on top of the graham cracker crust.

4 Cook in microwave for 1 minute. If cake is not done, heat an additional 15 seconds.

5 Top with mini marshmallows. If you have a kitchen torch, torch the marshmallows. You can also roast the marshmallows in the oven: Turn oven to 375 degrees F and heat mug for about 5 minutes, until marshmallow tops begin to turn light brown. Or, you can simply microwave the mug for another 15–30 seconds to melt the marshmallows, but you won't get the roasted appearance. Finish with a chocolate star, if desired. Cake is best consumed while still warm.

21-and-Over Mug Cakes

Most mug cakes in this book are kid-friendly. But occasionally, we just need some "adult time." This chapter adds a little alcohol to the ingredient list, producing tasty cakes that are for adults only. From a classy Champagne Cake to a festive Margarita to the über-decadent Kahlua Chocolate and Chocolate Stout cakes, these boozy mugfuls are perfect to serve at parties—including parties of one.

Baileys Irish Cream Cake

There's no hiding what's in your cake once this is finished cooking. One whiff and you'll immediately detect the Baileys Irish Cream. The sweet, creamy liqueur, so enjoyable on its own, is equally as tasty when flavoring this cake.

4 tbsp (30g) all-purpose flour

¼ tsp baking powder

1 tbsp (12.5g) granulated sugar

2 tbsp (30ml) fat-free milk

½ tbsp (7.5ml) vegetable oil

1 tbsp (15ml) Baileys Irish Cream

1 tbsp (11g) bittersweet chocolate chips

1 Combine all ingredients except chocolate chips in an oversized microwave-safe mug. Mix with a small whisk until batter is smooth. Stir in chocolate chips.

2 Cook in microwave for about 1 minute. If cake is not done, heat an additional 15 seconds. Let cake cool a few minutes. Cake is best consumed while still warm or within a few hours of it being cooked.

A Creamy Alternative

If you can get your hands on some cappuccino baking chips (found at specialty baking stores like King Arthur Flour), add those instead of chocolate chips for an even more intense creamy-coffee taste.

Kahlua Chocolate Cake

Chocolate and coffee are a match made in heaven, so you can only imagine how marvelous this cake tastes with its chocolate base and a whisper of coffee liqueur.

3 tbsp (22.5g) all-purpose flour

¼ tsp baking powder

2 tsp granulated sugar

2½ tbsp (37.5ml) fat-free milk

½ tbsp (7.5ml) vegetable oil

1 tbsp (7.5g) unsweetened cocoa powder (Dutch-processed)

1 tbsp (15ml) Kahlua coffee liqueur

1 Combine all ingredients in an oversized microwave-safe mug. Mix with a small whisk until batter is smooth.

2 Cook in microwave for about 1 minute. If cake is not done, heat an additional 15 seconds. Let cake cool a few minutes. Cake is best consumed while still warm or within a few hours of it being cooked.

Margarita Cake

This is another cake that's perfect for a party because it can be cooked directly in microwave-safe margarita glasses. You can even garnish the rim with some coarse sugar for the full effect!

4 tbsp (30g) all-purpose flour

¼ tsp baking powder

2 tbsp (25g) granulated sugar

2 tbsp (30ml) fat-free milk

½ tbsp (7.5ml) vegetable oil

½ tbsp (7.5ml) tequila

1 tsp triple sec

½ tbsp (7.5ml) fresh lime juice

¼ tsp lime zest

1 Combine all ingredients in an oversized microwave-safe mug. Mix with a small whisk until batter is smooth. You can cook batter directly in mug, or you can pour batter into a standard margarita glass.

2 Cook in microwave for about 1 minute. If cake is not done, heat an additional 15 seconds. Let cake cool a few minutes. Cake is best consumed while still warm or within a few hours of it being cooked.

Chocolate Stout Cake

Stout beer has quite the bitter aftertaste, but when paired with chocolate, it adds another dimension to the cake and enhances the bittersweet notes of the chocolate. The result is one very enjoyable cake.

3 tbsp (22.5g) all-purpose flour

¼ tsp baking powder

1 tbsp (12.5g) granulated sugar

2½ tbsp (37.5ml) fat-free milk

½ tbsp (7.5ml) vegetable oil

1 tbsp (7.5g) unsweetened cocoa powder (Dutch-processed)

1 tbsp (15ml) stout beer

TOPPING AND DECORATION, optional (serves 2)

½ cup (120ml) heavy whipping cream

2 tsp granulated sugar

chocolate syrup, for drizzling

chocolate chips, for sprinkling

1 Combine all ingredients in an oversized microwave-safe mug. Mix with a small whisk until batter is smooth.

2 Cook in microwave for about 1 minute. If cake is not done, heat an additional 15 seconds. Let cake cool a few minutes.

3 If desired, place the whipping cream and sugar in the mixing bowl of a stand mixer (or use a handheld mixer), and mix on high speed until peaks form. Top the cake with the whipped cream, drizzle over the chocolate syrup, and decorate with chocolate chips.

Piña Colada Cake

This tropical cocktail-inspired cake will leave you dreaming of beaches and paradise. It's flavored with rum, pineapples, and coconut milk.

4 tbsp (30g) all-purpose flour

¼ tsp baking powder

2 tbsp (25g) granulated sugar

3 tbsp (45ml) coconut milk

½ tbsp (7.5ml) vegetable oil

1 tbsp (15ml) dark rum

1 tbsp (13g) chopped canned pineapple (½-inch cubes)

CREAM CHEESE FROSTING, optional
(serves 2)

2 tbsp (28g) cream cheese

2 tbsp (28g) butter

5 tbsp (40g) confectioners' sugar, to taste

pineapple syrup, to drizzle

1 Combine all ingredients except pineapple cubes in an oversized microwave-safe mug. Mix with a small whisk until batter is smooth. Stir in pineapple.

2 Cook in microwave for about 1 minute. If cake is not done, heat an additional 15 seconds. Let cake cool a few minutes.

3 If desired, place the frosting ingredients in the mixing bowl of a stand mixer (or use a handheld mixer), and mix on high speed until light and fluffy. Top the cake with frosting and drizzle over pineapple syrup. Cake is best consumed while still warm or within a few hours of being cooked.

Rum Cake

Traditional rum cake is incredibly moist, as it is soaked in a rum glaze. This cake can be made without the glaze and is quite pleasing on its own, scented with rum and vanilla. But if you want the classic rum cake experience, I've included a recipe for a simple rum glaze—just cook it on the stovetop, then poke a few holes in your cake and pour it on.

CAKE

4 tbsp (30g) all-purpose flour

¼ tsp baking powder

1½ tbsp (19g) granulated sugar

3 tbsp (45ml) fat-free milk

½ tbsp (7.5ml) vegetable oil

½ tsp vanilla bean paste

1 tbsp (15ml) dark rum

RUM GLAZE (serves 2)

¼ cup (50g) granulated sugar

¼ cup (60ml) water

½ tbsp (7.5ml) dark rum

1 For the Cake: Combine all cake ingredients in an oversized microwave-safe mug. Mix with a small whisk until batter is smooth.

2 Cook in microwave for about 1 minute. If cake is not done, heat an additional 15 seconds. Let cake cool a few minutes while you prepare the rum glaze. Cake is best consumed while still warm or within a few hours of it being cooked.

3 For the Rum Glaze: Heat glaze ingredients in a small saucepan until it reduces and thickens. You can also make it in the microwave: Combine ingredients in a microwave-safe mug or bowl and heat at 1-minute intervals (pausing and checking in between) for about 3 to 4 minutes, until it bubbles and thickens. When glaze is ready, poke holes in cake and immediately pour it onto cake before it cools and hardens.

Champagne Cake

When you're in the mood to celebrate, this champagne-flavored cake is perfect party fare. The cake leaves a lingering fizzy sensation on your tongue from the champagne bubbles. Since champagne itself does not have much of a flavor, it's quite subtle in the cake. To help enhance the flavor, I suggest adding a dollop of champagne frosting.

CAKE

4 tbsp (30g) all-purpose flour

¼ tsp baking powder

1 tbsp (12.5g) granulated sugar

2 tbsp (30ml) fat-free milk

½ tbsp (7.5ml) vegetable oil

2 tbsp (30ml) dry champagne

FROSTING (serves 2)

½ cup (120g) heavy whipping cream

1 tbsp (15ml) dry champagne

2 tsp granulated sugar

1 For the Cake: Combine all cake ingredients in an oversized microwave-safe mug. Mix with a small whisk until batter is smooth.

2 Cook in microwave for about 1 minute. If cake is not done, heat an additional 15 seconds. Let cake cool a few minutes while you prepare the frosting. Cake is best consumed while still warm or within a few hours of it being cooked.

3 For the Frosting: While cake is cooling, combine frosting ingredients in a small bowl and mix on high speed with a hand mixer until peaks form. Add to top of cake before eating. The frosting makes enough for two cakes.

Suggestion:

This cake can be cooked directly in champagne flutes! Just pour batter into a standard-sized flute (microwave-safe), and make sure it only fills up about half of the glass (slightly more than half is okay, too). If you have too much, divide the batter into two servings and cook separately—just make sure to reduce cooking time for divided serving.

Mimosa Cake

Much like the popular brunch drink, this cake is flavored with champagne, orange juice, and a little orange liqueur to really bring out the orange essence. It will leave a faint bubbly sensation on your tongue. The cake tastes even better when you add a dollop of champagne frosting!

CAKE

4 tbsp (30g) all-purpose flour

¼ tsp baking powder

2 tbsp (25g) granulated sugar

1 tbsp (15ml) fat-free milk

½ tbsp (7.5ml) vegetable oil

2 tbsp (30ml) dry champagne

½ tbsp (7.5ml) triple sec

1 tbsp (15ml) orange juice

FROSTING (serves 2)

½ cup (120g) heavy whipping cream

1 tbsp (15ml) dry champagne

2 tsp granulated sugar

silver sprinkles, optional

1 For the Cake: Combine all cake ingredients in an oversized microwave-safe mug or champagne flute (see note below). Mix with a small whisk until batter is smooth.

2 Cook in microwave for about 1 minute. If cake is not done, heat an additional 15 seconds. Let cake cool a few minutes while you prepare the frosting. Cake is best consumed while still warm or within a few hours of it being cooked.

3 For the Frosting: While cake is cooling, combine frosting ingredients in a small bowl and mix on high speed with a hand mixer until peaks form. Add to the top of cake and decorate with silver sprinkles, if desired. The frosting makes enough for two cakes.

Fancier than a Mug!

This cake can be cooked directly in champagne flutes. Just pour batter into a standard-sized champagne flute (microwave-safe), and make sure it only fills up about half of the glass (slightly more than half is okay, too). If you have too much, divide the batter into two servings and cook separately (make sure to reduce cooking time for divided serving).

Sweet Beer Cake

While stout is more commonly used in desserts, this cake has a purer beer approach: light beer. You'll definitely taste the lingering yeast and hops in this sweet cake. Perfect for the beer lover with a sweet tooth!

4 tbsp (30g) all-purpose flour

¼ tsp baking powder

3 tsp granulated sugar

2 tbsp (30ml) fat-free milk

2 tbsp (30ml) light beer

1 Combine all ingredients in an oversized microwave-safe mug. Mix with a small whisk until batter is smooth.

2 Cook in microwave for about 1 minute. If cake is not done, heat an additional 15 seconds. Let cake cool a few minutes. Cake is best consumed while still warm or within a few hours of it being cooked.

Cookie Mug Cakes

There are days when I just *need* a cookie and a cake simply won't do. That's why I created a chapter dedicated to Cookie Mug Cakes. It's the same concept as the other mug cakes in this book, except the finished product is a warm, made-from-scratch cookie you can eat with a spoon.

These cakes have the firm, crisp texture of a cookie, so they won't rise up like cakes do. You can cook them in a mug, but they'll stay pretty flat at the bottom once they're finished. Fortunately, you can make these as traditional hand-held cookies: Just scoop the cookie dough out of the mug, place it on a microwave-safe plate lined with parchment paper, and form it into a cookie shape. It cooks up as a regular cookie!

These cakes taste best while they're still ooey-gooey and warm, so dive right in!

Chocolate Chip Cookie Cake

When it comes to cookies, my favorite is the good ol' chocolate chip. There's a reason why it's a classic. With this recipe, you can have this beloved American creation whenever you want.

1 tbsp (14g) butter

4 tbsp (30g) all-purpose flour

1 tbsp (12.5g) granulated sugar

1 tbsp (12.5g) light brown sugar

1 tbsp (15g) whisked egg (less than 1 egg)

¼ tsp vanilla extract

1 tbsp (11g) semisweet chocolate chips

1 Place butter in an oversized microwave-safe mug. Melt in microwave for about 40 seconds (for cold butter) or until completely melted.

2 Add remaining ingredients except chocolate chips. Mix with a small whisk until dough comes together. Stir in chocolate chips.

3 Press dough evenly across the bottom of the mug. Or, if you want to make a traditional cookie, scoop the batter out of the mug and form it into a cookie shape on a microwave-safe plate lined with parchment paper.

4 Cook in microwave for about 50 seconds. Let cookie cool a few minutes to firm up. Then eat immediately.

Cookies & Cream Cookie Cake

Having the word "cookie" in the name twice means it is extra yummy, right? This is a chewy cookie, with smatterings of cream and crushed crunchy chocolate Oreo pieces throughout.

1 tbsp (14g) butter

4 tbsp (30g) all-purpose flour

2 tbsp (25g) granulated sugar

1 tbsp (15g) whisked egg (less than 1 egg)

1 Oreo cookie

1 Place butter in an oversized microwave-safe mug. Melt in microwave for about 40 seconds (for cold butter) or until completely melted.

2 Add remaining ingredients except Oreo. Mix with a small whisk until dough comes together.

3 Add Oreo: Using a fork, smash Oreo into the dough until only small pieces of cookie remain.

4 Press dough evenly across the bottom of the mug. Or, if you want to make a traditional cookie, scoop the batter out of the mug and form it into a cookie shape on a microwave-safe plate lined with parchment paper.

5 Cook in microwave for about 50 seconds. Let cookie cool a few minutes to firm up. Then eat immediately.

Double Chocolate Chip Cookie Cake

If you're a chocoholic, you'll love this cookie thanks to its double dose of chocolate. It has a chocolate base and is studded with chocolate chips for an extra chocolate punch.

1 tbsp (14g) butter

3 tbsp (22.5g) all-purpose flour

2 tbsp (25g) light brown sugar

1 tbsp (15g) whisked egg (less than 1 egg)

1 tbsp (7.5g) unsweetened cocoa powder (Dutch-processed)

1 tbsp (11g) semisweet chocolate chips

1 Place butter in an oversized microwave-safe mug. Melt in microwave for about 40 seconds (for cold butter) or until completely melted.

2 Add remaining ingredients except chocolate chips. Mix with a small whisk until dough comes together. Stir in chocolate chips.

3 Press dough evenly across the bottom of the mug. Or, if you want to make a traditional cookie, scoop the batter out of the mug and form it into a cookie shape on a microwave-safe plate lined with parchment paper.

4 Cook in microwave for about 50 seconds. Let cookie cool a few minutes to firm up. Then eat immediately.

Oatmeal-Raisin Cookie Cake

This soft and chewy cookie has a healthy addition of rolled oats. It is loaded with raisins and dusted with cinnamon spice, just like the classic old-fashioned oatmeal cookie.

1 tbsp (14g) butter

1 tbsp (7.5g) all-purpose flour

2 tbsp (25g) light brown sugar

1 tbsp (15g) whisked egg (less than 1 egg)

3 tbsp (15g) old-fashioned oats

1/16 tsp ground cinnamon

1 tbsp (10g) raisins

1　Place butter in an oversized microwave-safe mug. Melt in microwave for about 40 seconds (for cold butter) or until completely melted.

2　Add remaining ingredients except raisins. Mix with a small whisk until dough comes together. Stir in raisins.

3　Press dough evenly across the bottom of the mug. Or, if you want to make a traditional cookie, scoop the batter out of the mug and form it into a cookie shape on a microwave-safe plate lined with parchment paper.

4　Cook in microwave for about 50 seconds. Let cookie cool a few minutes to firm up. Then eat immediately.

Peanut Butter Cookie Cake

⁓

This thick cookie is packed with peanut butter flavor. It's best consumed in small bites with a tall glass of milk.

1 tbsp (14g) butter

4 tbsp (30g) all-purpose flour

2 tbsp (25g) light brown sugar

1 tbsp (15g) whisked egg (less than 1 egg)

1 tbsp (16g) peanut butter

1 Place butter in an oversized microwave-safe mug. Melt in microwave for about 40 seconds (for cold butter) or until completely melted.

2 Add remaining ingredients. Mix with a small whisk until dough comes together.

3 Press dough evenly across the bottom of the mug. Or, if you want to make a traditional cookie, scoop the batter out of the mug and form it into a cookie shape on a microwave-safe plate lined with parchment paper.

4 Cook in microwave for about 50 seconds. Let cookie cool a few minutes to firm up. Then eat immediately.

Pudding Cookie Cake

This recipe adds a scoop of pudding mix powder to the dough for an extra-soft and moist chocolate chip cookie that practically melts in your mouth.

Note: Simply add the pudding mix powder as is. Do not make the mix into a pudding first.

1 tbsp (14g) butter

3 tbsp (22.5g) all-purpose flour

½ tbsp (6g) granulated sugar

1 tbsp (12.5g) light brown sugar

1 tbsp (15g) whisked egg (less than 1 egg)

1 tbsp (14g) instant vanilla pudding mix (or any flavor you like)

1 tbsp (11g) semisweet chocolate chips

1 Place butter in an oversized microwave-safe mug. Melt in microwave for about 40 seconds (for cold butter) or until completely melted.

2 Add remaining ingredients except chocolate chips. Mix with a small whisk until dough comes together. Stir in chocolate chips.

3 Press dough evenly across the bottom of the mug. Or, if you want to make a traditional cookie, scoop the batter out of the mug and form it into a cookie shape on a microwave-safe plate lined with parchment paper.

4 Cook in microwave for about 50 seconds. Let cookie cool a few minutes to firm up. Then eat immediately.

Sugar Cookie Cake

Sugar cookies are often overlooked, especially with their plain appearance. But, as the saying goes, appearances can be deceiving: This Sugar Cookie Cake is addictively delicious, with its soft and chewy texture and buttery finish.

1 tbsp (14g) butter

3 tbsp (22.5g) all-purpose flour

2 tbsp (25g) granulated sugar

1 tbsp (15g) whisked egg (less than 1 egg)

CREAM CHEESE FROSTING, optional
(serves 2)

2 tbsp (28g) cream cheese

2 tbsp (28g) butter

5 tbsp (40g) confectioners' sugar, to taste

sprinkles, if desired

1 Place butter in an oversized microwave-safe mug. Melt in microwave for about 40 seconds (for cold butter) or until completely melted.

2 Add remaining ingredients. Mix with a small whisk until dough comes together.

3 Press dough evenly across the bottom of the mug. Or, if you want to make a traditional cookie, scoop the batter out of the mug and form it into a cookie shape on a microwave-safe plate lined with parchment paper.

4 Cook in microwave for about 50 seconds. Let cookie cool a few minutes to firm up.

5 If desired, place the frosting ingredients in the mixing bowl of a stand mixer (or use a handheld mixer), and mix on high speed until light and fluffy. Spread the frosting directly on your mug cake or, using the cookie cutter of your choice, cut out an individual cookie or two. Spread the frosting on each cookie and decorate with sprinkles. Serve immediately.

Brownie Mug Cakes

As much as I enjoy my chocolate cakes, there is nothing that quite fills the void like a luscious brownie. I am a firm believer that a brownie should be chocolaty, dense, fudgy, and chewy. I don't want something that tastes like a cake; otherwise, I would just make a chocolate cake!

It's a little tricky to get the right texture when cooking with a microwave, but I've created some brownie variations that even the most devoted brownie buff will approve of. They won't have that crackly shiny surface that develops during baking, but they *will* taste just how a brownie should.

Unlike most of my mug cake recipes that I love eating straightaway, the brownies taste best if you give them about 30 minutes to settle. If you've ever made traditional brownies, you know that they need to cool completely to develop that chewy, dense, and fudgy texture. The same principle applies here. I know it's hard to have self-control when the brownie smells so mouthwatering after it's finished—but your patience will be rewarded.

Dulce de Leche Brownie Cake

❧

The rich, salty-sweet dulce de leche, derived from the caramelization of sweetened milk (and literally translated as "candy of milk"), turns this already luscious brownie into a true indulgence. You'll be in a sugary heaven after just one bite.

1 tbsp (14g) butter

2 tbsp (22.5g) semisweet chocolate chips

1 tbsp (7.5g) all-purpose flour

2 tbsp (30g) whisked egg (about half of 1 extra-large egg)

1 tbsp (15ml) plus 1 tbsp (15ml) dulce de leche (store-bought, see note below)

1 Place butter and chocolate chips in an oversized microwave-safe mug. Microwave for about 40 seconds and mix with a small whisk until chocolate is completely melted.

2 Add remaining ingredients except 1 tablespoon dulce de leche. Whisk until batter is smooth. Swirl in remaining dulce de leche with a fork.

3 Cook in microwave for about 1 minute. Let brownie cool about 30 minutes to allow it to set and become fudgy. Then eat immediately.

Where Do I Find It?

Dulce de leche is packaged in cans that resemble condensed milk. The most common brand, Nestlé, is found at most grocery stores in the international food aisle.

Cookies and Cream Blondie Cake

This blondie is speckled with crushed Oreos. The crunchy chocolate-cookie crumbles add another layer of texture to these chewy and fudgy treats.

1 tbsp (14g) butter

2 tbsp (15g) all-purpose flour

2 tbsp (25g) light brown sugar

2 tsp (10g) whisked egg (less than 1 egg)

1 Oreo cookie

1 Place butter in an oversized microwave-safe mug. Microwave for about 40 seconds (for cold butter) or until completely melted.

2 Add remaining ingredients except Oreo and mix with a small whisk until batter is smooth.

3 Add Oreo: Using a fork, smash Oreo into the batter until only small cookie pieces remain.

4 Cook in microwave for about 40 seconds. Let blondie cool about 30 minutes to allow it to set and become chewy. Then eat immediately.

Lava Brownie Cake

What's better than a rich, fudgy, chocolaty brownie? How about a rich, fudgy, chocolaty brownie with a gooey Nutella center? The silky hazelnut-chocolate filling makes for a blissful brownie experience.

1 tbsp (14g) butter

2 tbsp (22.5g) semisweet chocolate chips

1 tbsp (7.5g) all-purpose flour

2 tbsp (25g) granulated sugar

2 tbsp (30g) whisked egg (about half of 1 extra-large egg)

1 tbsp (18.5g) Nutella

TOPPING AND DECORATION, *optional* (serves 2)

½ cup (120ml) heavy whipping cream

2 tsp granulated sugar

1 tsp cocoa powder

chocolate shavings

1 Place butter and chocolate chips in an oversized microwave-safe mug. Microwave for about 40 seconds and mix with a small whisk until chocolate is completely melted.

2 Add remaining ingredients except Nutella and whisk until batter is smooth.

3 Place Nutella in the center of the batter and push down until it is no longer visible.

4 Cook in microwave for about 1 minute. Let brownie cool about 30 minutes to allow it to set and become fudgy. Then eat immediately.

5 If desired, place the whipping cream and sugar in the mixing bowl of a stand mixer (or use a handheld mixer), and mix on high speed until peaks form. Top the cake with whipped cream, sift over a little cocoa powder, and decorate with chocolate shavings. Serve immediately.

Blondie Cake

This is a classic blondie cake made with brown sugar and flour. Dense and chewy, it's perfect on its own or as a base for any add-ins you like, such as butterscotch or chocolate chips, coconut flakes, chopped nuts, or dried cherries.

1 tbsp (14g) butter

2 tbsp (15g) all-purpose flour

2 tbsp (25g) light brown sugar

2 tsp (10g) whisked egg (less than 1 egg)

1 Place butter in an oversized microwave-safe mug. Microwave for about 40 seconds (for cold butter) or until completely melted.

2 Add remaining ingredients and mix with a small whisk until batter is smooth.

3 Cook in microwave for about 40 seconds. Let blondie cool about 30 minutes to allow it to set and become chewy. Then eat immediately.

Nutella Brownie Cake

Do you enjoy the fudgy, chewy brownies you get with store-bought mixes? Well, I've managed to re-create that texture with this recipe: And it's even easier to make than the box mix! Ultra chewy, fudgy, chocolaty, and sweet, this brownie is as good as it gets.

2 tbsp (15g) all-purpose flour

2 tbsp (30g) whisked egg (about half of 1 extra-large egg)

¼ cup (74g) plus 1 tbsp (18.5g) Nutella

1 Combine all ingredients in an oversized microwave-safe mug. Mix with a small whisk until completely incorporated. Batter will be quite thick.

2 Cook in microwave for about 1 minute. Let brownie cool about 15 minutes to allow it to set and become chewy. Then eat immediately.

Classic Chocolate Brownie Cake

This is the quintessential brownie: fudgy, dense, chocolaty. If you like nuts in your brownies, go ahead and incorporate them or anything else you like. Or just devour it plain, which is the way I like my brownies best.

1 tbsp (14g) butter

2 tbsp (22.5g) semisweet chocolate chips

1 tbsp (7.5g) all-purpose flour

2 tbsp (25g) granulated sugar

2 tbsp (30g) whisked egg (about half of 1 extra-large egg)

1 Place butter and chocolate chips in an oversized microwave-safe mug. Microwave for about 40 seconds and mix with a small whisk until chocolate is completely melted.

2 Add remaining ingredients and whisk until batter is smooth.

3 Cook in microwave for about 1 minute. Let brownie cool about 30 minutes to allow it to set and become fudgy. Then eat immediately.

Spread Mug Cakes

I've already discussed my Nutella obsession and shared several luscious Nutella-based recipes in this book. But there are quite a few other equally delicious spreads out there that deserve some love, including peanut butter, cream cheese, and dulce de leche. These creamy toppings are so good, we may just want to eat them alone by the spoonful. But if you can spare enough for these cakes, you'll find that they are extra scrumptious with the addition of luxurious spreads.

Peanut Butter Cake

This is a dream cake for peanut butter fans: It's creamy, moist, and rich in peanut butter flavor.

4 tbsp (30g) all-purpose flour

¼ tsp baking powder

4 tsp granulated sugar

4 tbsp (60ml) fat-free milk

3 tbsp (48g) peanut butter

TOPPING AND DECORATION, *optional*

1 scoop of peanut brittle ice cream

Miniature milk chocolate flakes, to decorate

1 Combine all ingredients in an oversized microwave-safe mug. Mix with a small whisk until batter is smooth.

2 Cook in microwave for about 1 minute. If cake is not done, heat an additional 15 seconds. Let cake cool a few minutes. Cake is best consumed while still warm or within a few hours of it being cooked.

3 If desired, add a scoop of ice cream and decorate with miniature chocolate flakes.

Chocolate-Peanut Butter Cake

Chocolate and peanut butter make a happy marriage of flavors, and you can get two for the price of one when you use a chocolate-peanut butter spread. Chocolate-peanut butter is usually available at most national supermarket chains.

4 tbsp (30g) all-purpose flour

¼ tsp baking powder

4 tsp granulated sugar

4 tbsp (60ml) fat-free milk

3 tbsp (51g) chocolate-peanut butter

1 Combine all ingredients in an oversized microwave-safe mug. Mix with a small whisk until batter is smooth.

2 Cook in microwave for about 1 minute. If cake is not done, heat an additional 15 seconds. Let cake cool a few minutes. Cake is best consumed while still warm or within a few hours of it being cooked.

Pumpkin Butter Cake

Pumpkin butter used to be something I'd look forward to in the fall, but it's become so popular that it is now available year-round. This sweet-spice spread adds a little something extra to the already moist and buttery cake.

4 tbsp (30g) all-purpose flour

¼ tsp baking powder

1 tsp granulated sugar

2½ tbsp (37.5ml) fat-free milk

½ tbsp (7.5ml) vegetable oil

1 tbsp (18g) plus 1 tbsp (18g) pumpkin butter

1   Combine all ingredients except 1 tablespoon pumpkin butter in an oversized microwave-safe mug. Mix with a small whisk until batter is smooth.

2   Swirl in remaining pumpkin butter with a fork. Don't mix it in completely because you want to maintain swirls of pure gooey pumpkin butter.

3   Cook in microwave for about 1 minute. If cake is not done, heat an additional 15 seconds. Let cake cool a few minutes. Cake is best consumed while still warm or within a few hours of it being cooked.

Cheesecake

This cheesecake is full-blown creamy goodness. However, making a cheesecake in the microwave is a little tricky. The key to getting the right texture is letting the cake cool for several hours in the fridge, much like a traditional cheesecake. If you can't wait that long, you can eat it straightaway—it will still taste like a cheesecake but the texture won't be quite as dense and solidified.

CRUST

butter for greasing mug

4 tbsp (24g) finely ground graham cracker crumbs (about 1 sheet of graham crackers)

1 tbsp (14g) melted butter

CHEESECAKE

4 tbsp (56g) light cream cheese (or cream-cheese spread)

2 tbsp (30g) non-fat plain Greek yogurt

2½ tbsp (31g) granulated sugar

1 large egg, whisked

¼ tsp vanilla

½ tsp lime zest, grated

1 For the Crust: Grease the inside of an oversized microwave-safe mug with butter. Combine graham cracker crumbs and melted butter in mug and mix until butter completely coats the crumbs. Press down on the crumbs to form a crust evenly across the bottom of the mug.

2 For the Cheesecake: In a small bowl, combine all cheesecake ingredients except lime zest and mix with a small whisk until batter is smooth. If you are using cream cheese and not spread, there may be lumps left in the batter. In that case, use a bigger whisk, which should help you break up all the lumps. Pour batter into mug.

3 Cover top of mug with a paper towel or napkin and microwave for 1 minute. The cake should be mostly cooked, except in the center. Pause to check on it and make sure it's not overheating. Then heat in 20-second intervals (stopping to check your cake in between) for 1 minute. Cake should be completely cooked and pulling away from the mug. You don't want to microwave for the full 2 minutes at once because the batter may overheat and start popping and exploding in the microwave.

4 Gently slide the cheesecake out of the mug. (I let it come out upside-down onto a big spatula and then flip it back over onto a plate.)

5 Let cake cool a few minutes. When cake is no longer too hot to touch, place in fridge to cool and set for at least 1 hour. Garnish with lime zest.

Dulce de Leche Cake

This is one of my favorite mug cake recipes. Dulce de leche by itself is already out-of-this-world amazing. With gooey swirls throughout, each bite of cake is absolutely sublime.

4 tbsp (30g) all-purpose flour

¼ tsp baking powder

2 tsp granulated sugar

3 tbsp (45ml) fat-free milk

½ tbsp (7.5ml) vegetable oil

1 tbsp (15ml) dulce de leche (store-bought)

TOPPING AND DECORATION, optional (serves 2)

½ cup (120ml) whipping cream

2 tsp granulated sugar

1 tbsp (15ml) dulce de leche

chopped nuts

1 Combine all ingredients except dulce de leche in an oversized microwave-safe mug. Mix with a small whisk until batter is smooth.

2 Swirl in dulce de leche with a fork until it is barely incorporated. Don't mix it in completely because you want to maintain the gooey caramel swirls.

3 Cook in microwave for about 1 minute. If cake is not done, heat an additional 15 seconds. Let cake cool a few minutes.

4 If desired, place the whipping cream and sugar in the mixing bowl of a stand mixer (or use a handheld mixer), and mix on high speed until peaks form. Top the cake with whipped cream, drizzle over the dulce de leche, and sprinkle over chopped nuts. Cake is best consumed while still warm or within a few hours of being cooked.

Almond Butter Cake

Almonds make a healthy snack, so this cake is almost healthy, right? Okay, maybe not, but it is definitely nutty-licious. The cake is flavored with a triple dose of almonds: almond milk, almond butter, and raw almonds.

4 tbsp (30g) all-purpose flour

¼ tsp baking powder

2 tbsp (25g) granulated sugar

2 tbsp (32g) almond butter spread

4 tbsp (60ml) almond milk

4 to 5 raw almonds

1 Combine all ingredients except almonds in an oversized microwave-safe mug. Mix with a small whisk until batter is smooth. Sprinkle raw almonds on top.

2 Cook in microwave for about 1 minute. If cake is not done, heat an additional 15 seconds. Let cake cool a few minutes. Cake is best consumed while still warm or within a few hours of it being cooked.

Holiday Mug Cakes

The best part about holidays? It's the food, of course! I love the variety of festive foods centered around holiday celebrations—from Valentine's Day chocolate through Christmastime eggnog. This chapter features enticing holiday-themed desserts that you can easily whip up for a special occasion or any day of the year! If you're craving a wintry treat, try the Chocolate Peppermint or Gingerbread cake. When Easter rolls around, check out the Easter Surprise, which hides a melted chocolate egg at the center. For St. Patrick's Day, give the Guinness Chocolate Irish-Cream Cake a whirl. Great for groups and holiday parties, these cakes offer a fun, creative alternative to traditional desserts—and they're delicious, too!

Guinness Chocolate Irish-Cream Cake

Two popular alcoholic beverages that pop up during St. Patrick's Day are Guinness beer and Baileys Irish cream. This cake combines them both into one extra-scrumptious cake.

3 tbsp (22.5g) all-purpose flour

¼ tsp baking powder

2 tbsp (25g) granulated sugar

2 tbsp (30ml) fat-free milk

½ tbsp (7.5ml) vegetable oil

1 tbsp (7.5g) unsweetened cocoa powder (Dutch-processed)

1 tbsp (15ml) stout beer (preferably Guinness)

1 tbsp (15ml) Baileys Irish Cream

1 tsp confectioners' sugar, to decorate

1 Combine all ingredients except confectioners' sugar in an oversized microwave-safe mug. Mix with a small whisk until batter is smooth.

2 Cook in microwave for about 1 minute. If cake is not done, heat an additional 15 seconds. Let cake cool for a few minutes, and then sift the confectioners' sugar on top of the cake. Cake is best consumed while still warm or within a few hours of it being cooked.

Chocolate Peppermint Cake

My chocolate mug cake gets a winter makeover with the addition of crushed peppermint candies, giving a cool minty finish to each bite. It's also quite therapeutic to crush peppermint candies with a mallet—perfect relief for all that holiday stress!

¼ cup (45g) semisweet chocolate chips

3 tbsp (45ml) fat-free milk

3 tbsp (22.5g) all-purpose flour

¼ tsp baking powder

½ tbsp (7.5ml) vegetable oil

2 peppermint candies, finely crushed

TOPPING, optional
(serves 2)

½ cup (120ml) whipping cream

2 tsp granulated sugar

1 Combine chocolate chips and milk in an oversized microwave-safe mug. Microwave for about 40 seconds. Mix with a small whisk until chocolate is completely melted.

2 Add flour, baking powder, and oil and whisk until batter is smooth. Stir in crushed peppermints.

3 Cook in microwave for about 1 minute. If cake is not done, heat an additional 15 seconds. Let cake cool a few minutes. Cake is best consumed while still warm or within a few hours of it being cooked.

4 If desired, place the whipping cream and sugar in the mixing bowl of a stand mixer (or use a handheld mixer), and mix on high speed until peaks form. Top the cake with whipped cream. Cake is best consumed while still warm or within a few hours of being cooked.

Easter Surprise Cake

This simple white cake is studded with pastel sprinkles, giving it a festive Easter appearance. And what's Easter without an egg hunt? The clever cake also has a melted mini Cadbury egg hidden in the center!

4 tbsp (30g) all-purpose flour

¼ tsp baking powder

2 tsp granulated sugar

3 tbsp (45ml) fat-free milk

½ tbsp (7.5ml) vegetable oil

¼ tsp vanilla extract

½ tbsp (6g) pastel-colored sprinkles

1 mini Cadbury crème egg

TOPPING AND DECORATION,
optional (serves 2)

½ cup (120ml) whipping cream

2 tsp granulated sugar

green sprinkles

mini candy-coated chocolate eggs

1 Combine all ingredients except sprinkles and Cadbury egg in an oversized microwave-safe mug. Mix with a small whisk until batter is smooth.

2 Stir in sprinkles. Drop crème egg into the center of the batter and gently push down until batter barely covers the egg.

3 Cook in microwave for about 1 minute. If cake is not done, heat an additional 15 seconds. Let cake cool a few minutes. Cake is best consumed while still warm.

4 If desired, place the whipping cream and sugar in the mixing bowl of a stand mixer (or use a handheld mixer), and mix on high speed until peaks form. Top the cake with whipped cream, add the sprinkles, and decorate with the chocolate eggs. Cake is best consumed while warm.

Gingerbread Cake

This old-fashioned cake is spiced with molasses, cinnamon, and ground ginger. The taste is certain to evoke some wonderful winter memories.

4 tbsp (30g) all-purpose flour

¼ tsp baking powder

1 tbsp (12.5g) dark brown sugar

3 tbsp (45ml) fat-free milk

½ tbsp (7.5ml) vegetable oil

¼ tsp ground ginger

⅛ tsp ground cinnamon

½ tbsp (11g) dark molasses

1 Combine all ingredients in an oversized microwave-safe mug. Mix with a small whisk until batter is smooth.

2 Cook in microwave for about 1 minute. If cake is not done, heat an additional 15 seconds. Let cake cool a few minutes. Cake is best consumed while still warm or within a few hours of it being cooked.

Halloween Candy Cake

If you're looking for ways to use up leftover Halloween candy, check out this recipe: The chocolate cake base is made with plain chocolate bars, like Hershey's milk or dark chocolate. It's then studded with candies of your choice, such as Snickers, Reese's, and M&M's—whatever the trick-or-treaters have left behind!

¼ cup (1.5oz) chopped plain chocolate bars (like Hershey's milk or dark chocolate)

3 tbsp (45ml) fat-free milk

2 tbsp (15g) all-purpose flour

¼ tsp baking powder

½ tbsp (7.5ml) vegetable oil

2 tbsp chopped chocolate candies of your choice (like Snickers, Reese's, M&M's)

1   Combine chopped plain chocolate and milk in an oversized microwave-safe mug. Microwave for about 40 seconds. Mix with a small whisk until chocolate is completely melted.

2   Add flour, baking powder, and oil and whisk until batter is smooth. Stir in chopped candy.

3   Cook in microwave for about 1 minute. If cake is not done, heat an additional 15 seconds. Let cake cool a few minutes. Cake is best consumed while still warm or within a few hours of it being cooked.

Pumpkin Spice Cake

Throughout October and November, I'm obsessed with pumpkin everything! Pumpkin spice cake is one of my favorite fall-holiday treats, and this mug cake is a spot-on, one-serving replica of the popular cake.

4 tbsp (30g) all-purpose flour

¼ tsp baking powder

2 tbsp (25g) granulated sugar

2 tbsp (30ml) fat-free milk

½ tbsp (7.5ml) vegetable oil

2 tbsp (30g) pumpkin puree

⅛ tsp ground cinnamon

⅛ tsp ground nutmeg

1/16 tsp ground ginger

1/16 tsp ground cloves

1 Combine all ingredients in an oversized microwave-safe mug. Mix with a small whisk until batter is smooth.

2 Cook in microwave for about 1 minute 15 seconds. If cake is not done, heat an additional 15 seconds. Let cake cool a few minutes. Cake is best consumed while still warm or within a few hours of it being cooked.

Red Velvet Cake

❦

This alluring red-hued cake is perfect for Valentine's Day, Christmas, or any other red-themed holidays. The recipe contains all the traditional ingredients found in red velvet, including buttermilk, baking soda, vinegar, and a touch of cocoa powder. Each one plays an integral role in the distinctive, hard-to-describe red velvet flavor, the puffy texture, as well as the pretty red color—which I tried to create without using copious amounts of food coloring.

Note: Do not leave out any of the ingredients. People often try to omit the vinegar because they don't like the taste of it. But the vinegar is not added for taste. It interacts with the baking soda to make the cake fluffy and with the cocoa powder to bring out the red hue.

CAKE
- 4 tbsp (30g) all-purpose flour
- ⅛ tsp baking soda
- 2 tbsp (25g) granulated sugar
- 2 tbsp (30ml) buttermilk
- ½ tbsp (7.5ml) vegetable oil
- ½ tbsp (4g) unsweetened cocoa powder (Dutch-processed)
- ⅛ tsp distilled vinegar
- ¼ tsp red food coloring, plus more as needed to reach desired redness

CREAM CHEESE FROSTING, optional (serves 2)
- 2 tbsp (28g) cream cheese
- 2 tbsp (28g) butter
- 5 tbsp (40g) confectioners' sugar, to taste
- cocoa powder, for decoration

1 For the Cake: Combine all cake ingredients in an oversized microwave-safe mug. Mix with a small whisk until batter is smooth.

2 Cook in microwave for about 1 minute. If cake is not done, heat an additional 15 seconds. Let cake cool a few minutes while you prepare the frosting. Cake is best consumed while still warm or within a few hours of it being cooked.

3 For the Frosting: While cake is cooling, combine all frosting ingredients in a mixing bowl and whip on high speed until frosting is soft and fluffy. Sift a little cocoa powder to the top of the cake.

Eggnog Cake

Surprise your loved ones on Christmas morning with this easy and delicious eggnog mug cake. It's nonalcoholic, so kids can enjoy this spice cake as well.

*Note: You must use **cake flour** to get the right texture. Otherwise, it will have a much rougher texture and will not taste like a cake.*

2 tbsp (12.5g) cake flour (not all-purpose)

⅛ tsp baking powder

3 tsp granulated sugar

3 tbsp (45ml) light eggnog (store-bought)

1 Combine all ingredients in an oversized microwave-safe mug. Mix with a small whisk until batter is smooth.

2 Cook in microwave for about 1 minute. If cake is not done, heat an additional 15 seconds. Let cake cool a few minutes. Cake is best consumed while still warm or within a few hours of it being cooked.

Gluten-Free Mug Cakes

I receive a lot of requests for gluten-free recipes at *Kirbie's Cravings*, so I couldn't write a recipe book without including a chapter of delicious gluten-free options. The best part about these mug cakes is that you don't have to be living a gluten-free lifestyle to enjoy them, as they are some of the most sinfully rich recipes this book has to offer. From the Almond-Chocolate Torte to the Flourless Peanut Butter Cake to the Chocolate Mochi Cake, you'll be tempted to try them all!

For baking powder and all ingredients listed in this chapter, make sure the label clearly states that it's certified gluten-free.

Flourless Peanut Butter Cake

Unlike the other flourless cake recipes you'll find in this book, this cake does not come out dense at all. It cooks up quite fluffy, almost like a regular peanut butter cake, and anyone eating it will be surprised that there is no trace of flour.

2 tbsp (32g) peanut butter (store-bought)

⅛ tsp baking powder

1 tbsp (12.5g) granulated sugar

1 large egg

TOPPING AND DECORATION, *optional*

vanilla ice cream

caramel sauce

chocolate chips

1 Combine all ingredients in an oversized microwave-safe mug. Mix with a small whisk until batter is smooth and egg is fully beaten and incorporated.

2 Cook in microwave for about 1 minute. If cake is not done, heat an additional 15 seconds. Let cake cool about 30 minutes so the flavors fully develop.

3 Top the cake with a scoop of vanilla ice cream, drizzle over caramel sauce, and decorate with chocolate chips. Cake is best consumed within a few hours of it being cooked.

Chocolate Mochi Cake

Mochi is one of my favorite foods of all time. If you've never heard of it, mochi is a Japanese sweet that has a very chewy texture, and you can find it in traditional confectionary form or as mochi ice cream—a delicious ball of ice cream covered in chewy mochi. That unique texture is created through the use of glutinous rice flour (sometimes labeled "mochiko sweet rice flour"), which is found in most Asian grocery stores and in the Asian aisle of supermarkets. And despite what it sounds like, this "glutinous" rice flour is gluten-free. Chocolate is not a typical mochi flavor, but it's a wonderful fusion of cultures. This East-meets-West cake is chocolaty and chewy, reminiscent of a brownie.

2 tbsp (20g) glutinous (mochiko) rice flour (I use Koda Farms brand)

⅛ tsp baking powder

1 tbsp (12.5g) granulated sugar

2 tbsp (30ml) fat-free milk

½ tbsp (7.5ml) vegetable oil

½ tbsp (4g) unsweetened cocoa powder (Dutch-processed)

1   Combine all ingredients in an oversized microwave-safe mug. Mix with a small whisk until batter is smooth.

2   Cook in microwave for about 1 minute. If cake is not done, heat an additional 15 seconds. Let cake cool a few minutes. Cake is best consumed while still warm or within a few hours of it being cooked.

Almond-Chocolate Torte

Made with almond flour, this cake is a lesson in chocolate indulgence. The absence of gluten makes the chocolate flavor all the more rich and intense.

3 tbsp (21g) almond flour

¼ tsp baking powder

1 tbsp (12.5g) granulated sugar

2 tbsp (30ml) fat-free milk

1 tbsp (7.5g) unsweetened cocoa powder (Dutch-processed)

TOPPING AND DECORATION, optional (serves 2)

2 oz dark chocolate, chopped

¼ cup (60ml) heavy cream

flaked almonds, toasted

1 For the cake, combine all ingredients in an oversized microwave-safe mug. Mix with a small whisk until batter is smooth.

2 Cook in microwave for about 1 minute. If cake is not done, heat an additional 15 seconds. Let cake cool a few minutes.

3 For the frosting if desired, put the chopped dark chocolate in a small bowl. Then heat the heavy cream in a small pot. Once it begins to boil, remove from the stove. Pour the heavy cream over the chopped chocolate, and stir and mix until the chocolate is completely melted. Let the ganache cool and set (you can speed up this process by putting it in the fridge for about 45 minutes). You may need to stir it again to make it smooth and shiny.

4 Once the ganache is cooled, spread over the cake and then sprinkle with flaked almonds. Cake is best consumed within a few hours of being cooked.

Flourless Chocolate Cake

❧

I adore flourless cakes because they have such a deep chocolate flavor. This particular version requires just three ingredients to produce a decadent chocolate experience. Unlike most recipes in this book, this is one cake that needs to set for a few hours before you eat it—so plan ahead. If you eat it immediately after cooking, the chocolate flavor will still be quite light and the cake might taste almost eggy. But let it sit for a few hours and you'll be swooning with pleasure.

¼ cup (45g) semisweet chocolate chips

1 tbsp (15ml) vegetable oil

1 whisked egg

TOPPING AND DECORATION, optional (serves 2)

½ cup (120 ml) heavy whipping cream

2 tsp granulated sugar

1 tsp cocoa powder

chocolate shavings

1 Combine chocolate chips and oil in an oversized microwave-safe mug. Microwave for about 40 seconds. Mix with a small whisk until chocolate is completely melted.

2 Add whisked egg and whisk vigorously until batter is smooth and the egg is fully incorporated. Because the mixture is so dark, it will be hard to see if egg streaks remain. Lift your whisk a couple times to make sure you don't see evidence of unmixed egg still in the batter.

3 Cook in microwave for about 1 minute. Cake will look the slightest bit gooey on top, but as long as the cake has risen and is set, it should be ready. Let cake sit for several hours, so the chocolate flavor can fully develop and overcome any eggy taste.

4 Place the whipping cream and sugar in the mixing bowl of a stand mixer (or use a handheld mixer), and mix on high speed until peaks form. Top the cake with the whipped cream, sift over a little cocoa powder, and decorate with chocolate shavings.

Peanut Butter Banana Cake

I know, I know. There's already a flourless peanut butter cake in this book. So why am I sticking in another one? The banana adds a whole new dimension to the cake. Not only do bananas and peanut butter go hand in hand, but banana also gives this cake a denser texture, much like a classic flourless cake. For extra goodness, drizzle some salted caramel sauce on top.

Note: Make sure you scoop up 2 tablespoons of already-mashed banana, which is more than 2 tablespoons of unmashed banana cut from the fruit. The more overripe the banana, the easier it will be to whisk. Also, stay away from frozen bananas as they retain a great amount of water even after they are defrosted that will make the cake gummy.

2 tbsp (32g) peanut butter (store-bought)

¼ tsp baking powder

1 tbsp (12.5g) granulated sugar

2 tbsp (30g) whisked egg (about half of 1 extra-large egg)

2 tbsp (30g) mashed overripe banana (about half of a large banana)

caramel sauce (for serving; optional)

ice cream (for serving; optional)

1 Combine all ingredients in an oversized microwave-safe mug. Mix with a small whisk until batter is smooth.

2 Cook in microwave for about 1 minute. If cake is not done, heat an additional 15 seconds. Let cake cool a few minutes. Cake is best consumed while still warm or within a few hours of it being cooked.

3 If desired, drizzle caramel sauce over the cake or serve with a scoop of ice cream (or better yet, do both!).

Savory Mug Cakes

Does the idea of a savory cake scare you? Don't worry. You won't find recipes with any wacky flavor combinations here. Instead, this section shares cake-like creations that are meant to be savory—from Pizza Muffins to Chinese Buns to Cornbread. For those times when you aren't craving a sweet snack, here's a stroll down the savory lane.

Cheddar-Rosemary Cake

The fragrant piney herb pairs perfectly with almost any cheese, especially sharp cheddar. This fluffy cake is best eaten warm.

4 tbsp (30g) all-purpose flour

¼ tsp baking powder

4 tbsp (60ml) fat-free milk

½ tbsp (7.5ml) vegetable oil

⅛ tsp salt

½ tsp chopped fresh rosemary

2 tbsp (14g) shredded cheddar cheese

1 Combine all ingredients except rosemary and cheese in an oversized microwave-safe mug. Mix with a small whisk until batter is smooth. Stir in rosemary and cheese.

2 Cook in microwave for about 1 minute. If cake is not done, heat an additional 15 seconds. Let cake cool a few minutes. Cake is best consumed while still warm.

Cornbread Cake

This cornbread is unbelievably tender and moist—you may never want to make traditional cornbread again! It's perfect on its own or you can customize it however you wish. Sweeten it with honey, make it savory with bacon, or add spice with jalapenos. The possibilities are endless!

2 tbsp (15g) all-purpose flour

1/16 tsp baking soda

½ tbsp (6g) granulated sugar

2 tbsp (30ml) buttermilk

½ tbsp (7.5ml) vegetable oil

1 tbsp (15g) whisked egg (less than 1 egg)

2 tbsp (18g) cornmeal

1 Combine all ingredients in an oversized microwave-safe mug. Mix with a small whisk until batter is smooth.

2 Cook in microwave for about 1 minute. If cake is not done, heat an additional 15 seconds. Let cake cool a few minutes. Cake is best consumed while still warm or within a few hours of it being cooked.

Pizza Muffin Cake

❧

These Pizza Muffins come out looking super cute. On *Kirbie's Cravings*, there is a recipe for baked Pizza Cupcakes, which were a really big hit. I adapted those cupcakes to make a microwaveable, single-serving version, and this one is pretty close in terms of taste and texture.

You can prepare this in a mug, or cook it in a small ramekin (at least 6 ounces big so the batter doesn't overflow) to let the mini pepperoni and cheese on top really shine.

4 tbsp (30g) all-purpose flour

⅛ tsp baking powder

4 tbsp (60ml) fat-free milk

½ tbsp (7.5ml) vegetable oil

⅛ tsp salt

1 tsp Italian seasoning

1 tbsp (7g) plus 1 tbsp (7g) shredded mozzarella cheese

7 mini pepperoni plus another 7 for topping

marinara sauce (for serving)

basil leaf, optional

1 Combine all ingredients except mozzarella and pepperoni in an oversized microwave-safe mug. Mix with a small whisk until batter is smooth.

2 Stir in 1 tablespoon mozzarella and 7 mini pepperoni. If desired, pour batter into a 6-ounce ramekin for better presentation.

3 Sprinkle remaining 1 tablespoon mozzarella and 7 pepperoni on top of batter. Cook in microwave for about 1 minute. Sprinkle over a little Italian seasoning and garnish with a basil leaf, if desired. Eat warm with a side of marinara sauce.

Chinese Bun Cake

Chinese steamed buns come in several different forms. Sometimes they're sliced in half with pork slices sandwiched in between; sometimes they're filled with ground meat or a red barbeque pork meat; and other times they're served as plain buns that are eaten with a meal.

This recipe tastes remarkably similar to the plain bun. It has a very tight crumb and is slightly sweetened. It's placed in the savory chapter here because it is usually consumed with salty meats. Normally, the buns take a few hours of work: You have to proof them, roll them, and steam them. But this method takes only 5 minutes!

4 tbsp (30g) all-purpose flour

¼ tsp baking powder

3 tbsp (45ml) fat-free milk

1 tbsp (20g) condensed milk, plus extra for drizzling

edible gold leaf flakes, optional

1 Combine all ingredients in an oversized microwave-safe mug. Mix with a small whisk until batter is smooth.

2 Cook in microwave for about 1 minute. If cake is not done, heat an additional 15 seconds. Let cake cool for a few minutes.

3 This cake is considered savory, but if you wish to make it sweet, drizzle with the extra condensed milk and decorate with gold leaf flakes, if desired. Cake is best consumed while still warm or within a few hours of being cooked.

Bacon Beer Muffin Cake

Similar to a beer bread, but with a fluffier texture because it isn't baked for hours, this beer muffin carries a lingering trace of beer and bitter hops, balanced with savory smoky bacon.

4 tbsp (30g) all-purpose flour

¼ tsp baking powder

¼ tsp granulated sugar

3 tbsp (45ml) beer

½ tbsp (7.5ml) vegetable oil

1 tbsp (7g) shredded cheddar cheese

½ tbsp (about ½ slice) chopped pre-cooked bacon

1 Combine all ingredients except cheese and bacon in an oversized microwave-safe mug. Mix with a small whisk until batter is smooth. Stir in cheese and bacon.

2 Cook in microwave for about 1 minute. If cake is not done, heat an additional 15 seconds. Let cake cool a few minutes. Cake is best consumed while still warm or within a few hours of it being cooked.

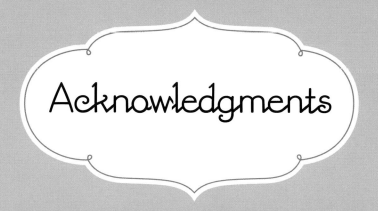

Acknowledgments

Writing this book has been a lifelong dream come true, but it is one that would never have come to be without the help of many, many people.

To Jeannine, thank you for taking a chance on me and for making this book a reality. To Sarah, I liked you the minute I first met you during a sushi dinner in San Diego (yes, I remember occasions based on the food). Despite the fact that we've only met a few times, you went above and beyond with your help and I am eternally grateful. To Lindsay, thank you for your keen eye, suggestions, and magical way with words. To my parents and siblings (Jessica, Kevin, and Cliff), thank you for always reading the blog, supporting it, and telling your friends about it, even when you don't always quite understand what I am doing. A special thank you to my sister, who also helped proofread my drafts. To my husband Donald, thank you for being my biggest supporter and for believing in me more than I do myself. And thank you for taste-testing every single one of the mug cakes made in writing this book.

And finally, a special thank you to all my readers. Thank you for all the emails, comments, ideas, and shares, or for just silently following along. You give me the motivation to continue to write, to create and to improve. Your support has helped me get here and without you, this book would not have been possible.